Discover ...

Shakespeare Plays
Series Editor: Klaus Hinz

William Shakespeare: Macbeth

Students' Book

Edited by Rainer Gocke and Angela Stock

Schöningh Verlag

W0309238

Sprachliche Betreuung: Neil Key

westermann GRUPPE

© 1999 Ferdinand Schöningh, Paderborn

© ab 2004 Bildungshaus Schulbuchverlage
Westermann Schroedel Diesterweg Schöningh Winklers GmbH
Braunschweig, Paderborn

www.schoeningh-schulbuch.de
Schöningh Verlag, Jühenplatz 1–3, 33098 Paderborn

Das Werk und seine Teile sind urheberrechtlich geschützt.
Jede Nutzung in anderen als den gesetzlich zugelassenen Fällen bedarf der vorherigen schriftlichen Einwilligung des Verlages.
Hinweis zu § 52a UrhG: Weder das Werk noch seine Teile dürfen ohne eine solche Einwilligung gescannt und in ein Netzwerk gestellt werden.
Dies gilt auch für Intranets von Schulen und sonstigen Bildungseinrichtungen.
Für Verweise (Links) auf Internet-Adressen gilt folgender Haftungshinweis:
Trotz sorgfältiger inhaltlicher Kontrolle wird die Haftung für die Inhalte der externen Seiten ausgeschlossen. Für den Inhalt dieser externen Seiten sind ausschließlich deren Betreiber verantwortlich. Sollten Sie daher auf kostenpflichtige, illegale oder anstößige Inhalte treffen, so bedauern wir dies ausdrücklich und bitten Sie, uns umgehend per E-Mail davon in Kenntnis zu setzen, damit beim Nachdruck der Verweis gelöscht wird.

Druck A[15] / Jahr 2018
Alle Drucke der Serie A sind im Unterricht parallel verwendbar.

Umschlaggestaltung: Nora Krull, Bielefeld, Foto: © defa
Druck und Bindung: westermann druck GmbH, Braunschweig

ISBN 978-3-14-**040041**-1

Contents

Getting started 4

Macbeth
• Act One 7
• Act Two 33
• Act Three 50
• Act Four 72
• Act Five 94

Con-Texts
• Witchcraft in *Macbeth*: The Weird Sisters 117
• Shakespeare's Language 118
• *Macbeth* in the Elizabethan Theatre. 121
• Tragedy 124
• Shakespeare and 'his' Time: The Order of the World 127

Glossary 130

Acknowledgements 136

An asterisk *in front of a word in the questions or the commentary means that it is explained in the Glossary at the end of the edition. An asterisk behind* a word in the text of the play means that it is explained in the margin on the same page.

Getting started

Valerie Wohlgemuth – her friends call her Val – is sitting in London's New Globe Theatre, opened in 1997 as a reconstruction of Shakespeare's Globe Theatre on the South Bank of the River Thames.

Her English teacher, Frau Beatrice Brückenbauer, has taken the 17 students of her *Leistungskurs* (LK) from Gelsenkirchen on a study tour to London. After about eight weeks of intensive study of Shakespeare's *Macbeth* – including various audio- and videotapes – the trip to Great Britain is a very welcome change for all the LK-members and their accompanying teachers, even more so as the journey provides them with an opportunity of meeting friends from their partner school at Sevenoaks in Kent.

Valerie in particular has developed a pretty special relationship with Ian Simpson, a sixth-former from their partner school. Ian ['iːən] thinks his teacher, Mr John Dixon, is a bit of a Shakespeare addict. For months he has treated his sixth form to *Othello, King Richard III, Much Ado About Nothing.* Yet to come: *Macbeth.* To introduce his students to this play and to celebrate the partnership with their friends from Gelsenkirchen, Mr Dixon has arranged a meeting of his sixth form and Frau Brückenbauer's LK at a performance of *Macbeth* in the New Globe. Ian, who has somewhat mixed feelings at the prospect of yet another Shakespeare play, has managed to sit next to Valerie.

From time to time we will listen to bits and pieces of the two friends' comments and remarks on the performance which is about to begin.

Inside the New Globe, 1997

A bird's-eye view of the Globe in 1607

The New Globe in its final phase of construction

Dramatis Personae/
The Persons in the Play
Macbeth ∞ Lady Macbeth
Victims:
King Duncan and his servants
Banquo
Lady Macduff and her children
Young Siward
Witches & Apparitions
Bystanders:
Ross
Lennox
Menteith
Angus
Caithness
Siward
Fleance, Banquo's son
Captain
An Old Man
Porter
Seyton
Gentlewoman
Doctor of physic
English doctor
Murderers, Lords,
Soldiers, Attendants,
Servants, Messengers
Surviving opponents:
Macduff, Thane of Fife
Malcolm, Duncan's son and future King of Scotland
Donaldbain,

Act One

Start here

What is the price of a dream?

The Tragedy of Macbeth asks the question as to how far people will go in order to achieve their prime ambition. What are they prepared to pay or to give up in order to see their most secret dream come true? What does it take, in the first place, to make them admit to themselves that they *have* this secret dream, this forbidden wish? And how do they afterwards deal with the fact that the price they have paid may have been too high?

1. Try to define or describe what the word 'ambition' means to you, what role it plays in people's lives, and whether you think it is a good or an evil force.
2. Taking historical or political figures as examples, discuss the relation between individual ambition and society in general. What impact can one person's ambition have on the people around him or her?
3. What, in your experience or opinion, is the relation between ambition and temptation, and between temptation and wrongdoing, or even crime?

Ellen Terry in the role of Lady Macbeth (1888), painted by J.S. Sargent

Act 1 Scene 1

Three women agree to meet Macbeth in a lonely place after the battle in which he has fought. Their words arouse the suspicion that they are in league with supernatural forces.

'When shall we three meet again?' From a 1981 production of Verdi's opera

Thunder and lightning. Enter three WITCHES

FIRST WITCH When shall we three meet again?
In thunder, lightning or in rain?

SECOND WITCH When the hurly burly's* done,
When the battle's lost, and won.

THIRD WITCH That will be ere* the set of sun.

FIRST WITCH Where the place?

SECOND WITCH Upon the heath.

THIRD WITCH There to meet with Macbeth.

FIRST WITCH I come, Graymalkin*.

SECOND WITCH Paddock* calls.

THIRD WITCH Anon*.

ALL Fair is foul, and foul is fair,
Hover through the fog and filthy air.

*Exeunt**

hurly-burly tumult, confusion (of a storm or a war)

ere before
Graymalkin a grey cat
Paddock a toad (Spirits serving witches often took the shapes of these animals.)
Anon At once
Exeunt Lat.: they leave (the stage)

Replace the adjectives 'fair/foul' by synonyms, e. g. 'good/evil', 'beautiful/ugly', 'honest/dishonest'. What is lost in comparison with Shakespeare's version? ➢

Activities

Shakespeare uses the first scene of every play to prepare the audience for the events to follow. In the case of *Macbeth,* the Weird Sisters' reversal of values has been called 'the key-note of the whole play'.

The play's 'motto'

1. What would happen in society, in families, in public and private life, if values were reversed and 'foul' was 'fair' and 'fair' was 'foul'?
2. Do you see any examples or evidence of such a reversal in the world around you?
   Be prepared for it at other dramatically important moments in the play!

Act 1 Scene 2

Messengers report to King Duncan that after long and hard battles, the rebels – led by Macdonald, the Norwegian king and the Thane of Cawdor – have been defeated. Macbeth has himself killed Macdonald; the king rewards him with Cawdor's lands and title.

'... and fixed his head upon our battlements.'

Alarum within*. Enter King* [DUNCAN], MALCOLM, DONALDBAIN, LENNOX, *with Attendants, meeting a bleeding* CAPTAIN

DUNCAN What bloody man is that? He can report,
As seemeth by his plight*, of the revolt
The newest state.

Alarum trumpet-call to battle
within behind the stage

As seemeth by his plight To judge from his wounds and exhaustion

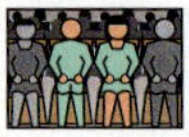

Ian: Who is that old chap in the white beard? Never tell me that's Macbeth! He doesn't look strong enough to hold a sword, let alone fight with it!
Val: That's the King of Scotland, actually. He doesn't need to fight, other people do it for him – Macbeth, for instance.

spent exhausted
choke their art prevent each other from using their swimming skills
kerns and galloglasses footsoldiers and horsemen (from Ireland and the Scottish islands)
with his brandished steel waving his sword over his head
minion darling
Which ne'er ... th'chaps Macbeth didn't lose time with polite greetings, but slit Macdonald open from the navel to the jaws.

MALCOLM This is the sergeant
Who like a good and hardy soldier fought
'Gainst my captivity. Hail, brave friend;
Say to the king, the knowledge of the broil
As thou didst leave it.

CAPTAIN Doubtful it stood,
As two spent* swimmers that do cling together
And choke their art*. The merciless Macdonald –
Worthy to be a rebel, for to that
The multiplying villainies of nature
Do swarm upon him – from the Western Isles
Of kerns and galloglasses* is supplied,
And Fortune on his damnèd quarrel smiling,
Showed like a rebel's whore. But all's too weak,
For brave Macbeth – well he deserves that name –
Disdaining Fortune, with his brandished steel*
Which smoked with bloody execution,
Like Valour's minion* carved out his passage
Till he faced the slave,
Which ne'er shook hands, nor bade farewell to him,
Till he unseamed him from the nave to th'chaps*
And fixed his head upon our battlements.

DUNCAN O valiant cousin, worthy gentleman.

As whence ... swells Often something that seems good is the source of trouble, just as the east is not only the place where the sun rises but also where storms gather.
trust their heels run away
furbished arms polished weapons

CAPTAIN As whence the sun 'gins his reflection,
Shipwrecking storms and direful thunders,
So from that spring whence comfort seemed to come,
Discomfort swells*. Mark, King of Scotland, mark,
No sooner justice had, with valour armed,
Compelled these skipping kerns to trust their heels*,
But the Norwegian lord, surveying vantage,
With furbished arms* and new supplies of men
Began a fresh assault.

DUNCAN Dismayed not this our captains, Macbeth and Banquo?

sooth truth

CAPTAIN Yes, as sparrows, eagles, or the hare, the lion.
If I say sooth*, I must report they were
As cannons over-charged with double cracks;
So they doubly redoubled strokes upon the foe.
Except they meant to bathe in reeking wounds
Or memorise another Golgotha,
I cannot tell.
But I am faint, my gashes cry for help.

The incomplete verse line ➤ leaves room for *stage business. How might an actor fill it?

DUNCAN So well thy words become thee as thy wounds;
They smack of honour both. Go get him surgeons.

[*Exit* Captain, attended*]

Exit Lat.: he leaves (the stage)

Enter ROSS *and* ANGUS

Who comes here?

Robert the Bruce, a 14th-century Scottish war hero. The equestrian statue can still be admired near Sterling, Scotland.

MALCOLM The worthy Thane* of Ross.

LENNOX What a haste looks through his eyes! So should he look
That seems to speak things strange.

ROSS God save the king.

DUNCAN Whence cam'st thou, worthy thane?

ROSS From Fife, great king,
Where the Norwegian banners flout the sky
And fan our people cold.
Norway* himself, with terrible numbers,
Assisted by that most disloyal traitor,
The Thane of Cawdor, began a dismal conflict,
Till that Bellona's* bridegroom, lapped in proof*,
Confronted him with self-comparisons*,
Point against point*, rebellious arm 'gainst arm,
Curbing his lavish spirit. And to conclude,
The victory fell on us –

DUNCAN Great happiness! –

ROSS That now Sweno,
The Norways' king, craves composition*.
Nor would we deign* him burial of his men
Till he disbursed at Saint Colm's Inch
Ten thousand dollars to our general use.

DUNCAN No more that Thane of Cawdor shall deceive
Our bosom interest*. Go pronounce his present* death
And with his former title greet Macbeth.

ROSS I'll see it done.

DUNCAN What he hath lost, noble Macbeth hath won.

Exeunt

Ian: Look, what does Shakespeare think he's doing? The second scene is almost over, and we haven't met either the hero or the heroine! In the other plays I've read, the most important characters appear more or less at the beginning, but here –? The first scene was complete gobbledigook, the second one is practically a news broadcast – this play is a bit slow in getting off the ground, isn't it?
Val: Why don't you just shut up and listen? By the way: ever heard of the 'indirect introduction of character'?

Thane Scottish clan chief

Norway King Sweno of Norway (A king *is* his country, so he is often called by its name rather than his own first name.)
Bellona the Roman goddess of war

≺ Who is 'Bellona's bridegroom'?

lapped in proof clothed in armour
Confronted … self-comparisons Faced him with skill and courage equal to his own
Point against point Sword against sword
craves composition begs for a peace treaty
deign allow

bosom interest absolute trust
present immediate

The last line echoes the Weird Sisters at the very beginning of the play (1.1.4). What exactly is ≺ being reversed here?

Activities

A country of warriors

The first thing we learn about Macbeth in this play is that he has recently committed acts of extreme violence.

1. Cite all the acts of violence Macbeth is reported to have committed.
2. What sort of imagery do the messengers use to describe these acts? Are these images positive or negative?
3. Does the description of the war help you to form an idea of King Duncan's Scotland, its values, its *ideologies, its self-image?

The erotics of war

In this scene, war is repeatedly personified as a woman who has a sexual relationship with Macbeth.

1. Can you find examples that are similar to 'Bellona's bride-groom' in line 54?
2. What is the effect of this *personification?

Act 1 Scene 3

While they are waiting for Macbeth, the three women talk about the black magic they have performed. When they meet Banquo and Macbeth, they prophesy future greatness to both men, who are not sure whether these creatures are women or demons, good or evil. When some of the prophecies come true right away, Macbeth decides to believe them.

Thunder. Enter the three WITCHES

FIRST WITCH Where hast thou been, sister?

SECOND WITCH Killing swine.

THIRD WITCH Sister, where thou?

This is the only instance in the whole play where one of the Weird Sisters is called 'witch'. How does she react?

FIRST WITCH A sailor's wife had chestnuts in her lap
And munched, and munched, and munched. 'Give me', quoth I.
'Aroint thee*, witch', the rump-fed ronyon* cries.
Her husband's to Aleppo gone, master o'th'Tiger*:
But in a sieve I'll thither sail,
And like a rat without a tail,
I'll do*, I'll do, and I'll do.

Aroint thee Get lost
rump-fed ronyon fat slut
Tiger (the name of a ship)

I'll do I'll work mischief

SECOND WITCH I'll give thee a wind.

FIRST WITCH Thou'rt kind.

THIRD WITCH And I another.

FIRST WITCH I myself have all the other,
And the very ports they blow,
All the quarters that they know
I'th'shipman's card.
I'll drain him dry as hay:
Sleep shall neither night nor day
Hang upon his penthouse lid*;
He shall live a man forbid.
Weary sennights* nine times nine,
Shall he dwindle, peak, and pine.
Though his bark* cannot be lost,
Yet it shall be tempest-tossed.
Look what I have.

penthouse lid eye lid (hanging above the eye like the roof above the wall of a house)
sennights seven-nights, i.e. a week
bark ship

SECOND WITCH Show me, show me.

FIRST WITCH Here I have a pilot's thumb,
Wrecked as homeward he did come.

Drum within

THIRD WITCH A drum, a drum;
Macbeth doth come.

ALL The weird* sisters, hand in hand,
Posters* of the sea and land,
Thus do go, about, about,
Thrice* to thine, and thrice to mine,
And thrice again, to make up nine.
Peace, the charm's wound up.

⋎ What are they doing?

weird from an Old English word for 'fate'. The three women have supernatural knowledge of the future.
Posters Fast travellers
Thrice Three times

Enter MACBETH *and* BANQUO

MACBETH So foul and fair a day I have not seen.

BANQUO How far is't called to Forres? What are these,
So withered and so wild in their attire,
That look not like th'inhabitants o'th'earth,
And yet are on't? – Live you, or are you aught*
That man may question? You seem to understand me,
By each at once her choppy finger laying
Upon her skinny lips; you should be women
And yet your beards forbid me to interpret
That you are so.

⋎ Underline all the phrases in Banquo's speeches that tell the other actors what to do and how to look (cf. *stage directions).

aught anything

MACBETH Speak if you can: what are you?

FIRST WITCH All hail Macbeth, hail to thee, Thane of Glamis*.

SECOND WITCH All hail Macbeth, hail to thee, Thane of
Cawdor.

Glamis [glɑ:mz]

'That shalt be king hereafter.' The first meeting as seen in Shakespeare's source history book and in a 1981 production of Verdi's opera

to start to jump or shudder

Val: They *sound* fair, that's right …
Ian: … but 'fair is foul'? Okay, I get it …

fair good
fantastical imaginary
great prediction i.e. you predict a great future for him
rapt amazed, stunned

THIRD WITCH All hail Macbeth, that shalt be king hereafter.

BANQUO Good sir, why do you start* and seem to fear
Things that do sound so fair*? – I'th'name of truth
Are ye fantastical*, or that indeed
Which outwardly ye show? My noble partner
You greet with present grace and great prediction*
Of noble having and of royal hope
That he seems rapt* withal. To me you speak not.
If you can look into the seeds of time
And say which grain will grow and which will not,
Speak then to me, who neither beg nor fear
Your favours nor your hate.

FIRST WITCH Hail.

SECOND WITCH Hail.

THIRD WITCH Hail.

FIRST WITCH Lesser than Macbeth, and greater.

SECOND WITCH Not so happy, yet much happier.

THIRD WITCH Thou shalt get* kings, though thou be none.
So all hail Macbeth and Banquo.

FIRST WITCH Banquo and Macbeth, all hail.

MACBETH Stay, you imperfect speakers. Tell me more.
By Sinel's* death, I know I am Thane of Glamis,
But how of Cawdor? The Thane of Cawdor lives
A prosperous gentleman, and to be king
Stands not within the prospect of belief*,
No more than to be Cawdor. Say from whence
You owe this strange intelligence*, or why
Upon this blasted heath you stop our way
With such prophetic greeting? Speak, I charge you.

Witches vanish

BANQUO The earth hath bubbles, as the water has,
And these are of them. Whither are they vanished?

MACBETH Into the air, and what seemed corporal,
Melted, as breath into the wind. Would* they had stayed.

BANQUO Were such things here as we do speak about?
Or have we eaten on the insane root*,
That takes the reason prisoner?

MACBETH Your children shall be kings.

BANQUO You shall be king.

MACBETH And Thane of Cawdor too: went it not so?

BANQUO To th'selfsame tune and words – who's here?

Enter ROSS *and* ANGUS

ROSS The king hath happily received, Macbeth,
The news of thy success, and when he reads
Thy personal venture* in the rebels' sight,
His wonders and his praises do contend
Which should be thine or his. Silenced with that,
In viewing o'er the rest o'th'selfsame day,
He finds thee in the stout Norwegian ranks,
Nothing afeard of what thyself didst make,
Strange images of death. As thick as tale
Came post* with post, and every one did bear
Thy praises in his kingdom's great defence,
And poured them down before him.

ANGUS We are sent
To give thee from our royal master thanks;
Only to herald* thee into his sight,
Not pay thee.

ROSS And for an earnest* of a greater honour,
He bade me, from him, call thee Thane of Cawdor:

Ian: What do they mean? I can't make head or tail of this!
Val: Shsh! Just wait and see!

to get to be the father of
Sinel Macbeth's father, from whom he inherited his title

Stands ... belief Is unbelievable

intelligence information

Would I wish

the insane root the root of a plant that causes hallucinations

➤ What is going on in the two men's minds in this short exchange?

A shift in meaning: Note that the adjective 'strange' used to mean more than simply 'odd'. In Elizabethan English, it had strong connotations of abnormality and unnaturalness. In *Macbeth,* the word comes up 20 times!

venture daring, courage

post message, messenger

herald escort

earnest token, promise

In which addition, hail most worthy thane,
For it is thine.

BANQUO What, can the devil speak true?

MACBETH The Thane of Cawdor lives. Why do you dress me
In borrowed robes?

ANGUS Who was the thane, lives yet,
But under heavy judgement bears that life
Which he deserves to lose.
Whether he was combined with those of Norway,
Or did line the rebel with hidden help
And vantage, or that with both he laboured
In his country's wrack*, I know not,
But treasons capital, confessed and proved,
Have overthrown him.

MACBETH [*Aside*] Glamis, and Thane of Cawdor:
The greatest is behind*. – Thanks for your pains*. –
[*To Banquo*] Do you not hope your children shall be kings,
When those that gave the Thane of Cawdor to me
Promised no less to them?

BANQUO That trusted home*,
Might yet enkindle* you unto the crown,
Besides the Thane of Cawdor. But 'tis strange,
And oftentimes, to win us to our harm,
The instruments of darkness tell us truths;
Win us with honest trifles, to betray's
In deepest consequence*. –
Cousins*, a word, I pray you.

MACBETH [*Aside*] Two truths are told,
As happy prologues to the swelling act
Of the imperial theme. – I thank you, gentlemen. –
This supernatural soliciting*
Cannot be ill*, cannot be good. If ill,
Why hath it given me earnest of success,
Commencing in a truth? I am Thane of Cawdor.
If good, why do I yield to that suggestion,
Whose horrid image doth unfix my hair
And make my seated heart knock at my ribs
Against the use of nature? Present fears
Are less than horrible imaginings*.
My thought, whose murder yet is but fantastical,
Shakes so my single state of man that function
Is smothered in surmise, and nothing is,
But what is not*.

BANQUO Look how our partner's rapt.

MACBETH If chance will have me king, why chance may
crown me
Without my stir*.

wrack ruin, downfall

The ... behind Kingship will follow
pains trouble

trusted home believed completely
to enkindle to excite your hopes

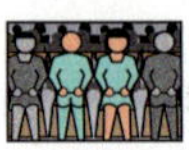

Val: Banquo is a clever man. Careful, too. I wish Macbeth would listen to him.
Ian: Why, what's Macbeth going to do? Is he actually going to top the old guy?
Val: Oh, getting interested, are we?

Win ... consequence Tell us truths in small matters in order to deceive us in important ones
Cousins (used for relatives of any kind)

What is this 'horrid image'? ➤

soliciting incitement, temptation
ill evil
Present ... imaginings Dangers that are really present are less frightening than fantasies.
My thought ... is not The mere thought of murder upsets me so much that my mind and body become disordered, and nothing seems real to me except my fantasies.
Without my stir Even if I remain passive

BANQUO New honours come upon him
Like our strange garments, cleave not to their mould,
But with the aid of use*.

New … use Like new clothes, his new titles make him feel uncomfortable until he gets used to them.

MACBETH Come what come may,
Time and the hour runs through the roughest day.

BANQUO Worthy Macbeth, we stay upon your leisure.

MACBETH Give me your favour*. My dull brain was wrought
With things forgotten. Kind gentlemen, your pains
Are registered where every day I turn
The leaf to read them. Let us toward the king.
[*To Banquo*] Think upon what hath chanced and at more time,
The interim having weighed it, let us speak
Our free hearts each to other*.

favour pardon

The interim … other Let us speak openly about these events when we have had more time to consider.

BANQUO Very gladly.

MACBETH Till then, enough. – Come, friends.

Exeunt

Activities

Casting magic spells

The Weird Sisters do not just look strange, they also sound different from the other characters in the play.

1. Describe their language in rhetorical terms. (The entries on *assonance, *blank verse and *rhyme in the Glossary will help you.)
2. Read lines 1.3.10-35 aloud: first one speaker, then three or more at the same time. Try to read in a singsong manner, emphasizing the rhyme and the rhythm. Move your bodies to accompany the words.
3. What sort of effect does the passage have on the speakers and the listeners?

Enter the hero

The first utterance of a character is usually of particular significance. Apply this to Macbeth.

Order begins to crumble

'… nothing is but what is not.'

1. What does Macbeth mean by this ominous remark?
2. Compare it to the Weird Sisters' announcement that 'fair is foul, and foul is fair', and discuss whether you think that the two *paradoxes mean something similar.
3. Find images expressing chaos, disorder or disintegration in this scene and link them to the two quotations above.

Inside Macbeth's mind

Macbeth seems to be in the habit of talking to himself when under pressure.

1. Look up the term *'aside' in the Glossary and explain its use in 1.3.
2. Macbeth begins a long aside in 1.3.126: does it end in 141, 143 or 146? Discuss the various possibilities.
3. What should the other characters onstage be doing while Macbeth is speaking aside?

'... that suggestion / Whose horrid image doth unfix my hair'. From Orson Welles' film (1948)

Act 1 Scene 4

The war is over

Bearing in mind what you have learnt about them so far, speculate for a moment on the meeting between Macbeth and his king. Remember it is the first meeting after the rebellion – and after the prophecy!

To celebrate the end of the war, King Duncan formally appoints his eldest son, Malcolm, heir to the throne. Macbeth, to whom it had been prophesied that *he* should be the next king of Scotland, is very upset by this turn of events. The idea of murdering the king takes firmer hold of him.

Flourish a fanfare of trumpets (here to announce the king)

Flourish. Enter King* [DUNCAN], LENNOX, MALCOLM, DONALDBAIN, *and Attendants*

DUNCAN Is execution done on Cawdor, or not
Those in commission yet returned?

liege lord

MALCOLM My liege*,
They are not yet come back. But I have spoke
With one that saw him die, who did report
That very frankly he confessed his treasons,
Implored your highness' pardon, and set forth
A deep repentance. Nothing in his life
Became him* like the leaving it. He died
As one that had been studied in his death,
To throw away the dearest thing he owed*
As 'twere a careless trifle*.

Became him Was appropiate to his rank as a nobleman
owed owned
trifle small, worthless thing

DUNCAN There's no art
To find the mind's construction in the face.*
He was a gentleman on whom I built
An absolute trust.

Enter MACBETH, BANQUO, ROSS, *and* ANGUS

O worthiest cousin,
The sin of my ingratitude even now
Was heavy on me. Thou art so far before,
That swiftest wing of recompense is slow
To overtake thee. Would thou hadst less deserved,
That the proportion both of thanks and payment
Might have been mine. Only* I have left to say,
More is thy due than more than all can pay.

MACBETH The service and the loyalty I owe,
In doing it, pays itself. Your highness' part
Is to receive our duties, and our duties
Are to your throne and state, children and servants,
Which do but what they should by doing everything
Safe toward your love and honour.

DUNCAN Welcome hither.
I have begun to plant thee and will labour
To make thee full of growing. Noble Banquo,
That hast no less deserved, nor must be known
No less to have done so, let me enfold thee
And hold thee to my heart.

BANQUO There if I grow,
The harvest is your own.

DUNCAN My plenteous joys,
Wanton in fullness, seek to hide themselves
In drops of sorrow*. Sons, kinsmen, thanes,
And you whose places are the nearest, know:

There's ... face One can't tell a person's character by his looks.

≺ Explain why this passage is a famous example of *dramatic irony.

Only All

drops of sorrow tears

'Sons, kinsmen, thanes …' From Orson Welles' film (1948)

We (pluralis maiestatis: Duncan is speaking formally.)
to establish our estate to settle the crown

Inverness Macbeth's castle
And … you As your guest I will be even more in your debt than I already am as your king.
harbinger messenger

What do these images ➤ reveal about Macbeth's feelings and intentions at this moment of disappointment?

to o'erleap to jump over
The eye … the hand Let me be blind to what I will do, i.e. kill the king.

peerless kinsman an incomparable family member (Historically, Macbeth was Duncan's cousin.)

***Stage directions** (SDs) printed in brackets do not appear in the original text of the play. They have been added by an *editor, who has prepared the play for modern readers to help them visualize the action.

We* will establish our estate* upon
Our eldest, Malcolm, whom we name hereafter
The Prince of Cumberland, which honour must
Not unaccompanied invest him only,
But signs of nobleness like stars shall shine
On all deservers [*To Macbeth*] From hence to Inverness*
And bind us further to you*.

MACBETH The rest is labour which is not used for you;
I'll be myself the harbinger* and make joyful
The hearing of my wife with your approach.
So humbly take my leave.

DUNCAN My worthy Cawdor.

MACBETH [*Aside*] The Prince of Cumberland: that is a step
On which I must fall down, or else o'erleap*,
For in my way it lies. Stars, hide your fires,
Let not light see my black and deep desires,
The eye wink at the hand*. Yet let that be,
Which the eye fears when it is done to see.

Exit

DUNCAN True, worthy Banquo, he is full so valiant,
And in his commendations I am fed;
It is a banquet to me. Let's after him,
Whose care is gone before to bid us welcome:
It is a peerless kinsman*.
Flourish

Exeunt

Activities

Court etiquette ➤

1. Simplify Duncan's, Macbeth's and Banquo's speeches into one short sentence each.
2. Why do they choose highly rhetorical and elaborate language to express themselves?

A royal gardener ➤

What do you make of the plant metaphors in lines 28-33? Include the family tree of the Scottish kings in your discussion.

Pedigree of the Royal Family of Scotland, including Banquo and James VI, i.e. James I of England, who reigned when *Macbeth* was written and performed for the first time

Act 1 Scene 5

Lady Macbeth has received a letter by her husband, in which he tells her of the Weird Sisters. She decides at once that they must murder Duncan to ensure that the prediction of kingship will come true. She is worried that Macbeth will have scruples and prepares herself by calling upon the powers of evil. When Macbeth arrives, he is evasive.

Enter the heroine ➤

Imagine possible settings for the following scene. There must be a contrast to the previous scenes.

Enter LADY MACBETH *alone, with a letter*

LADY MACBETH [*Reads*] 'They met me in the day of success, and I have learned by the perfectest report they have more in them than mortal knowledge*. When I burned in desire to question them further, they made themselves air, into which they vanished. Whiles I stood rapt in the wonder of it, came missives from the king who all-hailed me Thane of Cawdor, by which title before these weird sisters saluted me and referred me to the coming on of time, with 'Hail, king that shalt be.' This have I thought good to deliver thee, my dearest partner of greatness, that thou mightst not lose the dues of rejoicing* by being ignorant of what greatness is promised thee. Lay it to thy heart and farewell.'

Glamis thou art, and Cawdor, and shalt be
What thou art promised; yet do I fear thy nature,
It is too full o'th'milk of human kindness

mortal knowledge knowledge available to normal human beings

dues of rejoicing your share of happiness

Val: Hang on – this letter is not a complete account of Macbeth's encounter with the Weird Sisters!

'This have I thought good to deliver thee.' From a 1981 production of Verdi's opera

To catch the nearest way*. Thou wouldst* be great,
Art not without ambition, but without
The illness* should attend it. What thou wouldst highly,
That wouldst thou holily; wouldst not play false,
And yet wouldst wrongly win. Thou'dst have, great Glamis,
That which cries, 'Thus thou must do' if thou have it;
And that which rather thou dost fear to do,
Than wishest should be undone. Hie thee hither*,
That I may pour my spirits in thine ear
And chastise with the valour of my tongue
All that impedes thee from the golden round,
Which fate and metaphysical aid* doth seem
To have thee crowned withal.

Enter [ATTENDANT]

What is your tidings?

ATTENDANT The king comes here tonight.

LADY MACBETH Thou'rt mad to say it.
Is not thy master with him? Who, were't so,
Would have informed for preparation.

ATTENDANT So please you, it is true: our thane is coming.
One of my fellows had the speed of him;
Who almost dead for breath, had scarcely more
Than would make up his message.

LADY MACBETH Give him tending,
He brings great news.

Exit [*Attendant*]

The raven himself is hoarse,
That croaks the fatal entrance of Duncan
Under my battlements. Come, you spirits
That tend on mortal* thoughts, unsex* me here
And fill me from the crown* to the toe topfull
Of direst cruelty; make thick my blood,
Stop up th'access and passage to remorse
That no compunctious visitings of nature
Shake my fell* purpose nor keep peace between
Th'effect and it. Come to my woman's breasts
And take my milk for gall, you murd'ring ministers*,
Wherever in your sightless* substances
You wait on nature's mischief. Come, thick night,
And pall* thee in the dunnest* smoke of hell,
That my keen knife see not the wound it makes,
Nor heaven peep through the blanket of the dark,
To cry, 'Hold, hold.'

Enter MACBETH

Great Glamis, worthy Cawdor,
Greater than both by the all-hail hereafter,

To catch ... way To do the obvious thing, i.e. murder Duncan
Thou wouldst You would like to
illness unscrupulousness

Hie thee hither Come here quickly

metaphysical aid supernatural help

mortal murderous
to unsex to de-humanize
crown head (but with a *pun on a queen's crown)

Ian: This speech is like a prayer, isn't it? She's praying to devils and demons …!

fell savage, evil
ministers helpers
sightless invisible
pall wrap
dunnest darkest

Cite all words and images in this speech that evoke a sense of blackness or darkness.

Thy letters have transported me beyond
This ignorant present, and I feel now
The future in the instant.

What is the *tone of this exchange? Casual? Hesitant? Threatening?

MACBETH My dearest love,
Duncan comes here tonight.

LADY MACBETH And when goes hence?

MACBETH Tomorrow, as he purposes.

LADY MACBETH O never
Shall sun that morrow see.
Your face, my thane, is as a book where men
May read strange matters. To beguile the time,
Look like the time*, bear welcome in your eye,
Your hand, your tongue; look like th'innocent flower,
But be the serpent under't. He that's coming
Must be provided for, and you shall put
This night's great business into my dispatch*,
Which shall to all our nights and days to come
Give solely sovereign sway and masterdom.

To beguile ... the time In order to deceive the world, you have to conform to its expectations.

dispatch management (but also implying murder)

MACBETH We will speak further –

LADY MACBETH Only look up clear;
To alter favour ever is to fear*.
Leave all the rest to me.

Exeunt

Only ... fear Don't look so worried, or people will become suspicious.

Activities

Arguing with herself

Working in pairs, read out Lady Macbeth's first speech (13–28), but change it into a dialogue: read up to the first punctuation mark, then your partner takes over up to the next punctuation mark, and so on. Read it through several times this way.

1. What can you observe about the length of the individual phrases? Is there a development within the speech, and if so, what is its effect?
2. What is the difference between reading it as a monologue and as a dialogue?

The future queen of Scotland

In describing her husband, Lady Macbeth indirectly characterizes herself.

1. What impression do you have of her and of their marriage?
2. What is the textual evidence upon which you base your *characterization?
3. What role does the reversal of values (cf. 1.1.12) play here?

Preparing for murder

Lady Macbeth invokes the powers of darkness because she wants to transform herself.

1. Of what nature is this transformation, and why does she think it necessary?
2. Discuss the meaning of the word 'unsex'.

The hero at home

So far, we have seen Macbeth in his roles as warrior and subject to his king. In this scene we hear him described by his wife, and quite a different man seems to appear.

1. Compare your previous notions of him with the notion his wife has of him.
2. Can the two be reconciled, or do they pose an irreconcilable contradiction?

Act 1 Scene 6

Hautboys, and Torches. Enter* King [Duncan], Malcolm,

With great politeness and courtesy, Lady Macbeth welcomes King Duncan and his thanes as her guests. Duncan praises the beauty and peacefulness of the castle and the landscape, and very elaborately thanks her for her hospitality.

Donaldbain, Banquo, Lennox, Macduff, Ross, Angus, *and Attendants*

Duncan This castle hath a pleasant seat*; the air
Nimbly and sweetly recommends itself
Unto our gentle senses.

Banquo This guest of summer,

Hautboys Oboes
seat location

What is the dramatic effect of Duncan and Banquo's description of Macbeth's castle and its surroundings?

'This castle has a pleasant seat ...' Glamis Castle as it was reconstructed in the 19th century

The temple-haunting martlet*, does approve
By his loved mansionry that the heaven's breath
Smells wooingly here. No jutty, frieze,
Buttress, nor coign of vantage but this bird
Hath made his pendent bed* and procreant cradle;
Where they most breed and haunt, I have observed
The air is delicate.

Enter LADY [MACBETH]

DUNCAN See, see, our honoured hostess. – The love
That follows us sometime is our trouble,
Which still we thank as love. Herein I teach you
How you shall bid God yield* us for your pains
And thank us for your trouble.

LADY MACBETH All our service,
In every point twice done and then done double,
Were poor and single business to contend
Against those honours deep and broad wherewith
Your majesty loads our house. For those of old,
And the late* dignities heaped up to them,
We rest* your hermits*.

DUNCAN Where's the Thane of Cawdor?
We coursed him at the heels* and had a purpose
To be his purveyor*, but he rides well,
And his great love, sharp as his spur, hath holp* him
To his home before us. Fair and noble hostess,
We are your guest tonight.

LADY MACBETH Your servants ever

temple-haunting martlet housemartin, a bird that likes to nest in the walls of churches

pendent bed hanging nest

to yield to reward

late recent
to rest to remain
hermits holy people at prayer
coursed ... heels followed closely behind him
purveyor servant who announces the arrival of a king and organizes meals
holp helped

'All our service ...' From a BBC film (1982)

Have theirs, themselves, and what is theirs in count
To make their audit at your highness' pleasure,
Still to return your own.

DUNCAN Give me your hand;
Conduct me to mine host: we love him highly
And shall continue our grace towards him.
By your leave*, hostess.

Exeunt

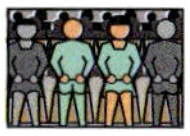

Ian: Macbeth is at home, isn't he? Why doesn't he join his wife to welcome the king?

By your leave If you allow (A polite phrase: perhaps Duncan is taking Lady Macbeth's arm to lead her into the castle.)

Activities

Welcoming the royal victim

Comment on Lady Macbeth's language and manner in this scene with regard to:

1. her language and manner in the previous scene,
2. her husband's language and manner in 1.4.

Act 1 Scene 7

After dinner, the Macbeths quarrel over the intended murder. Macbeth's sense of honour and his fear of punishment keep him back; but when his wife accuses him of being a weakling and plans the murder in greater detail, he is won over by her.

An actor's opinion

Macbeth knows at once, the minute he sees the first witch, what is going to happen. The interesting part of the play is that the man has imagination and the woman has none. The man sees it all, she does not. That's what gives her the enormous courage to plot the whole thing, force him into it, persuade him.'
(Sir Laurence Olivier, cf. ill. on pp. 29 and 36)
Judith Cook, *Shakespeare's Players*, Harrap, London, 1983, p. 148

This statement implies that his vivid imagination makes Macbeth hesitate, while her lack of imagination allows Lady Macbeth to press on. Try to make sense of this view by discussing the role of imagination in the plotting of a murder.

Sewer Head servant at a meal
divers ['daivəz] several

List the rational and the irrational elements in Macbeth's struggle to decide whether to murder his king.

If … come If the single act of murder were all that is necessary (i.e. to achieve the crown), and if there were no further consequences to be feared, I would not care for life after death.

that in that, in as much as

Hath … meek Has been such a mild king

taking-off murder

Striding the blast Standing above the storm
sightless couriers invisible (and blind) winds

Hautboys. Torches. Enter a Sewer and divers* Servants with dishes and service over the stage. Then enter* MACBETH

MACBETH If it were done when 'tis done, then 'twere well
It were done quickly. If th'assassination
Could trammel up the consequence and catch
With his surcease, success, that but this blow
Might be the be-all and the end-all – here,
But here, upon this bank and shoal of time,
We'd jump the life to come.* But in these cases,
We still have judgement here that* we but teach
Bloody instructions, which being taught, return
To plague th'inventor. This even-handed justice
Commends th'ingredience of our poisoned chalice
To our own lips. He's here in double trust:
First, as I am his kinsman and his subject,
Strong both against the deed; then, as his host,
Who should against his murderer shut the door,
Not bear the knife myself. Besides, this Duncan
Hath borne his faculties so meek*, hath been
So clear in his great office, that his virtues
Will plead like angels, trumpet-tongued against
The deep damnation of his taking-off*.
And pity, like a naked newborn babe
Striding the blast*, or heaven's cherubin horsed
Upon the sightless couriers* of the air,
Shall blow the horrid deed in every eye,
That tears shall drown the wind. I have no spur

'Pity, like a naked newborn babe …' Detail from an engraving by William Blake (1757–1827)

To prick the sides of my intent, but only
Vaulting ambition which o'erleaps itself
And falls on th'other –*

Enter Lady [Macbeth]

How now? What news?

Lady Macbeth He has almost supped. Why have you left the chamber?

Macbeth Hath he asked for me?

Lady Macbeth Know you not he has?

Macbeth We will proceed no further in this business.
He hath honoured me of late, and I have bought
Golden opinions from all sorts of people,
Which would be worn now in their newest gloss,
Not cast aside so soon.

Lady Macbeth Was the hope drunk
Wherein you dressed yourself? Hath it slept since?
And wakes it now to look so green and pale*
At what it did so freely? From this time,
Such I account thy love. Art thou afeard
To be the same in thine own act and valour,
As thou art in desire? Wouldst thou have that
Which thou esteem'st the ornament of life*,
And live a coward in thine own esteem,
Letting I dare not wait upon I would,
Like the poor cat i'th'adage*?

'We will proceed no further'. Laurence Olivier and Vivien Leigh in a 1955 London theatre production

I have no ... th'other My ambition is the only thing that incites me to murder; but like an over-eager rider, I may fall and ruin everything.

The reasons he gives his wife are not the ones he listed when he was alone. What is he hiding from her, and why?

What psychological strategies does Lady Macbeth use to put pressure on her husband?

green and pale sick with hangover

the ornament of life the crown

adage proverb ('The cat would [i.e. wanted to] eat fish but dared not get her feet wet.')

Prithee I beg you ('I pray thee')
become be suitable for

MACBETH Prithee*, peace.
I dare do all that may become* a man,
Who dares do more is none.

to break to suggest, mention
durst dared

Did then adhere Were perfect (for the murder)

They … you Now that time and place are right for the murder, you lose your nerve.

given suck fed a baby with the milk from my breasts

Absence of emotion or excess of it? Cold-blooded cruelty or horrified despair?

LADY MACBETH What beast was't then
That made you break* this enterprise to me?
When you durst* do it, then you were a man.
And to be more than what you were, you would
Be so much more the man. Nor time, nor place
Did then adhere*, and yet you would make both.
They have made themselves and that their fitness now
Does unmake you*. I have given suck* and know
How tender 'tis to love the babe that milks me:
I would, while it was smiling in my face,
Have plucked my nipple from his boneless gums
And dashed the brains out, had I so sworn
As you have done to this.

MACBETH If we should fail?

wassail feasting
convince overpower
quell slaughter

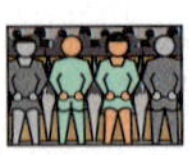

Val: Have you noticed that the Macbeths have stopped using King Duncan's name?
Ian: Yes, and they never spell out the fact that they are going to murder him.

LADY MACBETH We fail?
But screw your courage to the sticking-place,
And we'll not fail. When Duncan is asleep,
Whereto the rather shall his day's hard journey
Soundly invite him, his two chamberlains
Will I with wine and wassail* so convince*
That memory, the warder of the brain,
Shall be a fume, and the receipt of reason
A limbeck only. When in swinish sleep
Their drenchèd natures lies as in a death,
What cannot you and I perform upon
Th'unguarded Duncan? What not put upon
His spongy officers, who shall bear the guilt
Of our great quell*?

MACBETH Bring forth men-children only,
For thy undaunted mettle should compose
Nothing but males. Will it not be received,
When we have marked with blood those sleepy two
Of his own chamber and used their very daggers,
That they have done't?

LADY MACBETH Who dares receive it other,
As we shall make our griefs and clamour roar
Upon his death?

Collect all the *euphemisms for 'murder' or 'to kill' that come up in their conversation, and discuss whether they make a difference to the atmosphere of the scene.

MACBETH I am settled and bend up
Each corporal agent to this terrible feat.
Away, and mock the time with fairest show,
False face must hide what the false heart doth know.

Exeunt

Activities

Psychomachia

Choose one member of the class to be Macbeth's Bad Angel, persuading him to murder Duncan, and another to be his Good Angel, trying to prevent him from doing so.

1. Speak your arguments in turn, as you find them in this speech (you can use your own words if you like) – and remember that you are fighting for his soul!
2. Act out this struggle by choosing someone to play Macbeth: the Bad and the Good Angel each take an arm and pull Macbeth over to his or her side as they speak their arguments in turn. Be as serious and determined as possible!
3. What do you think might happen to someone in this kind of mental torment?

God and Evil fighting for man's soul. From the Hours (Prayer book) of Catherine of Cleves

Voice and meaning

In Elizabethan writing and printing, the question mark was used for questions as well as for emphatic statements (exclamations).
Read the short exchange in line 59 aloud and try out the different meanings it can have, depending on the punctuation and your tone of voice.

Draw a metaphor

What difficulties would you encounter if you attempted to draw a picture or make a short film of the images in the lines 21–5? Include William Blake's famous engraving (ill. on p. 28) in your discussion.

Reviewing Act One

The playwright

Inform yourselves about William Shakespeare.

1. What do you know of him, his life, his times, and his reputation?
2. Have you heard of any Shakespeare plays other than the one you are reading? Which ones? In what form did you encounter them?
3. How do you feel about reading *Macbeth* at school?

The themes and images

'Shakespeare introduces every dominant theme, every significant image, in the first few scenes of a play – the rest is merely an unfolding of the implications.'
Apply this statement to the first act of *Macbeth* and try to identify themes or images which you think might be significant in the following acts.
It is impossible to be precise in this exercise – you are encouraged to use your imagination and intuition!

The characters

1. Who – speaking in terms of *plot and *action – are the most important people in act one? Why?
2. Can you speculate on their further involvement in the plot?
3. Describe and characterize their relations with each other. Which are the most important relationships so far?

The language

Quote three very short passages (1-5 lines) which you take to be the most significant, beautiful, or for other reasons the most memorable ones of the opening act.

1. Justify your choices and discuss alternatives in class.
2. Analyse the rhetorical figures employed in your chosen lines. (The rhetorical terms explained in the Glossary will come in useful.) You are encouraged to repeat this particular exercise after each act.

Disguise and identity

Val: These New Globe people are really serious about authenticity, aren't they? Even the female characters are played by boys, just as they were in Shakespeare's days!
Ian: I must say, it does take some getting used to, as far as I'm concerned … But it's cool, somehow!

1. What difference does it make if a female character is played by a male actor – as it invariably was in the Elizabethan theatre?
2. Which plays or films have you seen in which a woman was played by a man or vice versa?
3. What seem to be the most fascinating, problematic, or comic aspects of *cross-dressing?

Act Two

Start here

To kill a king

The violent death of a public figure always upsets people and creates anxiety.

1. Inform yourselves about the contexts and the effects of the murders of 20th-century political leaders, e.g. Mahatma Gandhi, John F. Kennedy, Martin Luther King or Jizak Rabin.
2. Discuss whether the murder the Macbeths are planning can be compared to politically motivated assassinations.

28 June 1914: The Austrian Prince Franz Ferdinand is shot in Sarajevo by a Serbian terrorist.

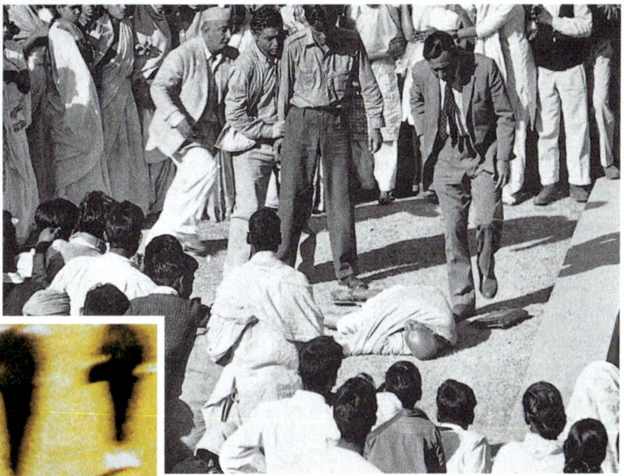

30 January 1948: Mahatma Gandhi is killed by a Hindu fanatic.

22 November 1963: John F. Kennedy is assassinated. Rumours of an involvement of the CIA have not died down.

Act 2 Scene 1

On their way to bed, Banquo and his son Fleance meet Macbeth, who tries to find out whether Banquo would side with him against Duncan. Banquo makes it very clear that he will not betray the king and that he distrusts the Weird Sisters.
Left alone, Macbeth has a hallucination: a blood-stained dagger seems to lead him to Duncan's bedroom. He follows it.

Enter BANQUO, *and* FLEANCE *with a Torch*[*-bearer*] *before him*

BANQUO How goes the night, boy?

FLEANCE The moon is down; I have not heard the clock.

BANQUO And she* goes down at twelve.

FLEANCE I take't, 'tis later, sir.

BANQUO Hold, take my sword. – There's husbandry in heaven*,
Their candles are all out. – Take thee that too.
A heavy summons lies like lead upon me,
And yet I would not sleep; merciful powers,
Restrain in me the cursèd thoughts that nature
Gives way to in repose*.

Enter MACBETH, *and a Servant with a torch*

Give me my sword –
Who's there?

MACBETH A friend.

BANQUO What, sir, not yet at rest? The king's abed.
He hath been in unusual pleasure
And sent forth great largess* to your offices*.
This diamond he greets your wife withal,
By the name of most kind hostess, and shut up*
In measureless content.

MACBETH Being unprepared,
Our will became the servant to defect,
Which else should free have wrought.

BANQUO All's well.
I dreamed last night of the three weird sisters;
To you they have showed some truth.

MACBETH I think not of them;
Yet when we can entreat an hour to serve,
We would spend it in some words upon that business,
If you would grant the time.

she (In English, the moon is feminine, the sun masculine.)
There's … heaven The angels are saving money (i.e. no stars are out)
A heavy … repose Although I'm very tired I dare not sleep because I'm afraid I'll dream of the Weird Sisters' prophecy.

What are the 'cursèd thoughts' that come to Banquo when he is asleep?

Val: I must say, I find this very confusing, the way they keep bringing torches onto the stage in broad daylight.
Ian: Yes, but isn't it a brilliant way to let the audience know about the setting of the scene?

What are the torches for? What other clues can you pick up, apart from the torches, to help you picture the scene in your mind's eye?

largess presents, reward
offices servant's quarters
shut up went to bed

BANQUO At your kind'st leisure*.

MACBETH If you shall cleave to my consent*, when 'tis,
It shall make honour for you.

BANQUO So I lose none
In seeking to augment it, but still keep
My bosom franchised* and allegiance clear,
I shall be counselled*.

MACBETH Good repose the while.

BANQUO Thanks, sir; the like to you,

[*Exeunt*] *Banquo* [*Fleance, and Torch-bearer*]

MACBETH [*To Servant*] Go bid thy mistress, when my drink is ready,
She strike upon the bell. Get thee to bed.

Exit [*Servant*]

Is this a dagger which I see before me,
The handle toward my hand? Come, let me clutch thee:
I have thee not, and yet I see thee still.
Art thou not, fatal vision, sensible
To feeling as to sight*? Or art thou but
A dagger of the mind, a false creation,
Proceeding from the heat-oppressèd* brain?
I see thee yet, in form as palpable*
As this which now I draw.
Thou marshall'st* me the way that I was going,
And such an instrument I was to use.
Mine eyes are made the fools o'th'other senses,
Or else worth all the rest. I see thee still
And on thy blade and dudgeon* gouts* of blood,
Which was not so before. There's no such thing:
It is the bloody business which informs
Thus to mine eyes. Now o'er the one half-world
Nature seems dead*, and wicked dreams abuse
The curtained sleep. Witchcraft celebrates
Pale Hecate's* off'rings, and withered murder,
Alarmed by his sentinel*, the wolf,
Whose howl's his watch, thus with his stealthy pace,
With Tarquin's ravishing strides, towards his design*
Moves like a ghost. Thou sure and firm-set earth,
Hear not my steps, which way they walk, for fear
Thy very stones prate* of my whereabout,
And take the present horror from the time,
Which now suits with it. Whiles I threat*, he lives;
Words to the heat of deeds too cold breath gives.

A bell rings

I go, and it is done. The bell invites me.
Hear it not, Duncan, for it is a knell*
That summons thee to heaven or to hell. *Exit*

At … leisure Whenever you want

cleave … consent do what I want

bosom franchised mind free from guilt
So I … counselled I'll follow you, provided that you intend no crime.

Art … sight? Can I not touch as well as see you?

heat-oppressèd feverish (and hallucinating)
palpable touchable

marshall'st guide (i.e. to Duncan's bedroom, but figuratively also to damnation)
dudgeon handle
gouts drops

What is the effect of Macbeth's addressing the dagger?

What does Macbeth mean when he says 'Nature seems dead'?

Nature seems dead It is dark
Hecate goddess of witchcraft (She appears in 3.5 and 4.1.)
sentinel watch(man)
design purpose
to prate to tell
to threat to threaten
knell funeral bell

The Roman king **Tarquin** raped and mutilated his friend's wife, Lucrece. To Elizabethans, he was a symbol of betrayal and cruelty.

Activities

Partners or rivals?

Consider the exchange between Macbeth and Banquo (9–30) in the light of the fact that these are two men who share a worrying, perhaps even dangerous, secret.

1. Do they actually behave that way?
2. Try to spell out the *subtext of their exchange: the play gives you the lines they *speak*, but what are the lines they are *thinking?*

Temptation or hallucination?

In the Middle Ages and the Renaissance it was believed that the devil could create illusions in order to lead people into temptation:

> 'Why should it be [impossible] for the devil and his angels [...] to conjure up fantastic images for deluding the human senses, whereby they can deceive men, whether awake or asleep, or rouse them to frenzy?'
> (Augustinus, *De Trinitate*, IV.xi. 14)

1. List all the words in Macbeth's 'dagger soliloquy' (2.1.33-64) that have to do with sensual perception, then the ones that have to do with illusions or hallucinations.
2. How does Macbeth try to explain his vision?
3. Discuss the supernatural explanations that would offer themselves to an Elizabethan audience. Are there any words or ideas in the speech that remind you of the Weird Sisters?

'Come, let me clutch thee.' Laurence Olivier in a 1955 London theatre production

Act 2 Scene 2

Having drugged Duncan's servants, Lady Macbeth has left it to her husband to commit the murder. When they meet, Macbeth is almost out of his mind with horror at what he has done. Lady Macbeth has to take charge of the situation.

Enter LADY [MACBETH]

LADY MACBETH That which hath made them drunk, hath made me bold;
What hath quenched them, hath given me fire.
[*An owl shrieks*]
Hark, peace!
It was the owl that shrieked, the fatal bellman
Which gives the stern'st good-night. He is about it*.
The doors are open, and the surfeited grooms*
Do mock their charge with snores. I have drugged their possets,
That death and nature do contend about them*,
Whether they live, or die.

Enter MACBETH [*with two bloody daggers*]

MACBETH Who's there? What ho?

LADY MACBETH Alack, I am afraid they have awaked,
And 'tis not done; th'attempt and not the deed
Confounds* us – hark – I laid their daggers ready,
He could not miss 'em. Had he* not resembled
My father as he slept, I had done't. My husband?

MACBETH I have done the deed. Didst thou not hear a noise?

LADY MACBETH I heard the owl scream and the crickets cry.
Did not you speak?

MACBETH When?

LADY MACBETH Now.

MACBETH As I descended?

LADY MACBETH Ay.

MACBETH Hark, who lies i'th'second chamber?

LADY MACBETH Donaldbain.

MACBETH This is a sorry* sight.

LADY MACBETH A foolish thought, to say a sorry sight.

MACBETH There's one did laugh in's sleep, and one cried, 'Murder!',

He … it Macbeth is at this moment committing the murder.
surfeited grooms drunken servants

them Duncan's servants

Lady Macbeth's short speech is full of fearful thoughts, not fully expressed. Take each sentence or half-sentence and identify the thought or feeling behind it.

Confounds Ruins
he Duncan

What is 'a sorry sight'?

sorry miserable, awful

That they did wake each other; I stood, and heard them,
But they did say their prayers and addressed them
Again to sleep.

LADY MACBETH There are two lodged together.

MACBETH One cried 'God bless us!' and 'Amen' the other,
As* they had seen me with these hangman's* hands.
List'ning their fear, I could not say 'Amen'
When they did say 'God bless us.'

As As if

hangman executioner (who often had to cut bodies into pieces before or after they were dead)

LADY MACBETH Consider it not so deeply.

MACBETH But wherefore could not I pronounce 'Amen'?
I had most need of blessing and 'Amen'
Stuck in my throat.

LADY MACBETH These deeds must not be thought
After these ways; so, it will make us mad.

MACBETH Methought I heard a voice cry, 'Sleep no more:
Macbeth does murder sleep', the innocent sleep,
Sleep that knits up the ravelled sleeve of care,
The death of each day's life, sore labour's bath,
Balm of hurt minds, great nature's second course*,
Chief nourisher in life's feast.

second course main course in a meal

LADY MACBETH What do you mean?

Ian: Quite right, what does he mean? Could we have that speech again, preferably in plain English?

MACBETH Still it cried, 'Sleep no more' to all the house;
'Glamis hath murdered sleep', and therefore Cawdor
Shall sleep no more. Macbeth shall sleep no more.

LADY MACBETH Who was it, that thus cried? Why, worthy, thane,
You do unbend* your noble strength to think
So brain-sickly of things. Go get some water
And wash this filthy witness from your hand.
Why did you bring these daggers from the place?
They must lie there. Go carry them and smear
The sleepy grooms with blood.

to unbend to relax, grow weak

MACBETH I'll go no more.
I am afraid to think what I have done;
Look on't again, I dare not.

Val: Isn't this a bit thin-skinned, for a warrior whose 'brandished steel / [...] smoked with bloody execution' (1.2.17) only a few days ago?

LADY MACBETH Infirm of purpose!
Give me the daggers. The sleeping and the dead
Are but as pictures; 'tis the eye of childhood
That fears a painted devil. If he do bleed,
I'll gild* the faces of the grooms withal,
For it must seem their guilt. *Exit*

to gild to cover with a layer of gold

*Knock within**

within behind the stage

MACBETH Whence is that knocking?
How is't with me, when every noise appals me?

'Give me the daggers.' Vivien Leigh in a 1955 London theatre production

What hands are here? Ha: they pluck out mine eyes.
Will all great Neptune's ocean wash this blood
Clean from my hand? No: this my hand will rather
The multitudinous seas incarnadine*,
Making the green one red.

Enter LADY [MACBETH]

LADY MACBETH My hands are of your colour, but I shame
To wear a heart so white*.

Knock [*within*]

I hear a knocking
At the south entry. Retire we to our chamber;
A little water clears us of this deed.
How easy is it then! Your constancy
Hath left you unattended.*

Knock [*within*]

Hark, more knocking.
Get on your night-gown, lest occasion call us
And show us to be watchers*. Be not lost
So poorly in your thoughts.

MACBETH To know my deed, 'twere best not know myself.

Knock [*within*]

Wake Duncan with thy knocking: I would thou couldst.

Exeunt

to incarnadine to make red

white cowardly

Your ... unattended You have lost your nerve.

watchers awake

A Name the two images or ideas with which Macbeth, like one in shock, has become obsessed.

Activities

The murderer's wife

The murder has not succeeded according to Lady Macbeth's plans.

1. What has gone wrong?
2. Speculate on her thoughts and feelings after she has gone back to her bedroom.

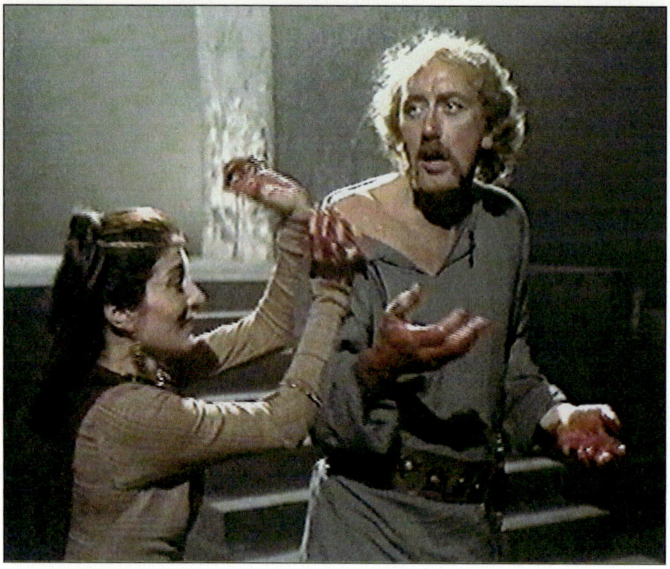

'Be not lost so poorly in your thoughts.' From a BBC film (1982)

Sound effects

Imagine you were turning 2.2 into a radio-play.

1. What sounds, apart from the speeches of the actors, are mentioned or implied?
2. Read through the scene: two of you are Macbeth and Lady Macbeth, the rest are responsible for the sound effects.

Act 2 Scene 3

The Porter answers Macduff's and Lennox's knocking at the gate. He is in a drunkenly playful mood and imagines he is the gatekeeper of hell, letting in different kinds of sinners.
Macduff finds Duncan murdered in his bed. In the ensuing chaos, Macbeth kills the drugged servants, claiming he was too furious to control himself. Afraid that they might be the next victims, Duncan's sons escape from the castle.

Enter a PORTER. *Knocking within*

PORTER Here's a knocking indeed: if a man were porter of hell-gate, he should have old turning the key. *(Knock)* Knock, knock, knock. Who's there i'th'name of Beelzebub? Here's a farmer that hanged himself on th'expectation of plenty*.

< Who is Beelzebub?

on the ... plenty i.e. on seeing that the harvest would be good, and the corn he had hoarded last year would be worthless

The **Gunpowder Plot** (5 November 1605) may provide a context for the Porter's remarks: Among the conspirators was a Jesuit priest who used the name 'Farmer' as an alias. In his trial, he maintained that it was permissible by God's law to tell half-truths ('equivocations') in self-defence.

'Entrance to Hell' from 'The Last Judgement', Guild Chapel at Stratford-upon-Avon (made from what survived in 1807)

Faith (a mild oath)
equivocator double-dealer

stealing i.e. stealing cloth
goose pressing iron

the primrose … bonfire the easy, pleasurable way to hell

carousing drinking

Marry (mild oath, shortened form of 'by the Virgin Mary')
Lechery Sexual lust

mars destroys
him i.e. lechery
stand to stand to attention like a soldier (with a *pun on 'have an erection')
equivocates tricks
giving … lie 1) lying to him, 2) making him fall down (with dizziness)

I … him i.e. I proceeded to throw him out (by throwing up)

Val: Those Elizabethans must have had a very odd sense of humour to find this character funny! I don't even understand half of the things he's saying!

Can you imagine what Shakespeare's audience enjoyed about the speeches of the Porter? What are the topics of his jokes?

Come in time – have napkins enough about you, here you'll sweat for't. *(Knock)* Knock, knock. Who's there in th'other devil's name? Faith*, here's an equivocator* that could swear in both the scales against either scale, who committed treason enough for God's sake, yet could not equivocate to heaven. O, come in, equivocator. *(Knock)* Knock, knock, knock. Who's there? Faith, here's an English tailor come hither for stealing* out of a French hose. Come in, tailor, here you may roast your goose*. *(Knock)* Knock, knock. Never at quiet: what are you? But this place is too cold for hell. I'll devil-porter it no further: I had thought to have let in some of all professions that go the primrose way to th'everlasting bonfire*. *(Knock)* Anon, anon. I pray you, remember the porter. [*Opens door*]

Enter MACDUFF *and* LENNOX

MACDUFF Was it so late, friend, ere you went to bed,
That you do lie so late?

PORTER Faith, sir, we were carousing* till the second cock, and drink, sir, is a great provoker of three things.

MACDUFF What three things does drink especially provoke?

PORTER Marry*, sir, nose-painting, sleep, and urine. Lechery*, sir, it provokes, and unprovokes: it provokes the desire, but it takes away the performance. Therefore much drink may be said to be an equivocator with lechery: it makes him, and it mars* him*, it sets him on, and it takes him off; it persuades him and disheartens him, makes him stand to* and not stand to. In conclusion, equivocates* him in a sleep, and giving him the lie*, leaves him.

MACDUFF I believe drink gave thee the lie last night.

PORTER That it did, sir, i'the very throat on me, but I requited him for his lie, and, I think, being too strong for him, though he took up my legs sometime, yet I made a shift to cast him*.

Enter MACBETH

MACDUFF Is thy master stirring?
Our knocking has awaked him: here he comes.
[*Exit Porter*]

LENNOX Good morrow, noble sir.

MACBETH Good morrow, both.

MACDUFF Is the king stirring, worthy thane?

MACBETH Not yet.

MACDUFF He did command me to call timely on him;
I have almost slipped the hour.

MACBETH I'll bring you to him.

MACDUFF I know this is a joyful trouble to you, but yet 'tis one.

MACBETH The labour we delight in physics* pain. This is the door.

MACDUFF I'll make so bold to call, for 'tis my limited service.
Exit

LENNOX Goes the king hence today?

MACBETH He does – he did appoint so.

LENNOX The night has been unruly: where we lay,
Our chimneys were blown down, and, as they say,
Lamentings heard i'th'air, strange screams of death
And prophesying with accents terrible
Of dire combustion* and confused events,
New hatched to th'woeful time. The obscure bird*
Clamoured the livelong night. Some say, the earth
Was feverous and did shake.

MACBETH 'Twas a rough night.

LENNOX My young remembrance cannot parallel
A fellow to it.

Enter MACDUFF

MACDUFF O horror, horror, horror,
Tongue nor heart cannot conceive, nor name thee.

MACBETH *and* LENNOX What's the matter?

MACDUFF Confusion* now hath made his masterpiece:
Most sacrilegious murder hath broke ope*
The Lord's anointed temple* and stole thence
The life o'th'building.

MACBETH What is't you say, the life?

LENNOX Mean you his majesty?

MACDUFF Approach the chamber and destroy your sight
With a new Gorgon*. Do not bid me speak:
See and then speak yourselves.
Exeunt Macbeth and Lennox
Awake, awake!
Ring the alarum bell! Murder and treason!
Banquo and Donaldbain! Malcolm, awake,
Shake off this downy sleep, death's counterfeit,
And look on death itself. Up, up, and see
The great doom's image. Malcolm, Banquo,
As from your graves rise up and walk like sprites*
To countenance this horror.

Bell rings. Enter LADY [MACBETH]

LADY MACBETH What's the business
That such a hideous trumpet calls to parley*
The sleepers of the house? Speak, speak.

physics heals

dire combustion terrible chaos
obscure bird night-owl

➤ What is the *tone of Macbeth's reply?

Confusion Chaos
ope open
anointed temple i.e. the body of King Duncan and, figuratively, the kingdom. (A king was anointed by having sacred oil spread on his head at his coronation.)

Gorgon female monster in Greek mythology, with snakes for hair. Her sight turned people into stones.

sprites spirits, ghosts

parley meeting

The repetition … fell If I repeated this bad news to a woman, it would kill her.

MACDUFF O gentle lady,
'Tis not for you to hear what I can speak.
The repetition in a woman's ear
Would murder as it fell*. –

Enter BANQUO

O Banquo, Banquo,
Our royal master's murdered.

LADY MACBETH Woe, alas.
What, in our house?

BANQUO Too cruel, anywhere.
Dear Duff, I prithee contradict thyself
And say it is not so.

Enter MACBETH *and* LENNOX

Appearance vs. reality: Is ➤ Macbeth merely acting the shocked host, or is he expressing his sincerest, innermost feelings?

chance event

All … toys Everything is worthless and insignificant.

MACBETH Had I but died an hour before this chance*,
I had lived a blessèd time, for from this instant,
There's nothing serious in mortality.
All is but toys*; renown and grace is dead,
The wine of life is drawn, and the mere lees
Is left this vault to brag of.

Enter MALCOLM *and* DONALDBAIN

amiss wrong

DONALDBAIN What is amiss*?

MACBETH You are, and do not know't.
The spring, the head, the fountain of your blood
Is stopped, the very source of it is stopped.

MACDUFF Your royal father's murdered.

MALCOLM O, by whom?

LENNOX Those of his chamber, as it seemed, had done't.
Their hands and faces were all badged with blood,
So were their daggers which, unwiped, we found
Upon their pillows. They stared and were distracted;
No man's life was to be trusted with them.

MACBETH O, yet I do repent me of my fury
That I did kill them.

MACDUFF Wherefore did you so?

expedition force, speed

the pauser, reason reason, which should make one pause and consider before one acts

MACBETH Who can be wise, amazed, temp'rate, and furious,
Loyal and neutral, in a moment? No man.
Th'expedition* of my violent love
Outran the pauser, reason*. Here lay Duncan,
His silver skin laced with his golden blood
And his gashed stabs looked like a breach in nature,
For ruin's wasteful entrance. There the murderers,
Steeped in the colours of their trade; their daggers
Unmannerly breeched with gore. Who could refrain,

'Look to the lady.' From a 1955 London theatre production

That had a heart to love and in that heart
Courage to make's love known?

LADY MACBETH Help me hence, ho.

MACDUFF Look to the lady.

[*Exit Lady Macbeth, helped*]

MALCOLM [*To Donaldbain*] Why do we hold our tongues, that most may claim
This argument for ours?

DONALDBAIN [*To Malcolm*] What should be spoken here,
Where our fate hid in an auger hole* may rush
And seize us? Let's away. Our tears are not yet brewed.

MALCOLM [*To Donaldbain*] Nor our strong sorrow upon the foot of motion*.

BANQUO Look to the lady,
And when we have our naked frailties* hid
That suffer in exposure, let us meet
And question this most bloody piece of work
To know it further. Fears and scruples* shake us:
In the great hand of God I stand and thence
Against the undivulged pretence* I fight
Of treasonous malice.

MACDUFF And so do I.

ALL So all.

MACBETH Let's briefly put on manly readiness
And meet i'th'hall together.

Val: Very clever of her to faint at just this point, isn't it?
Ian: Why, do you think she's faking it? No, I think she's horrified, and the strain is too much for her.

auger-hole very small hole in a wall

upon … motion ready to be expressed

naked frailties half-dressed bodies (and, metaphorically, their vulnerability to violence)

scruples doubts

undivulged pretence hidden purpose

ALL Well contented.
Exeunt [all but Malcolm and Donaldbain]

MALCOLM What will you do? Let's not consort with them.
To show an unfelt sorrow is an office
Which the false* man does easy*. I'll to England.

false treacherous
easy easily, without guilt

DONALDBAIN To Ireland, I. Our separated fortune
Shall keep us both the safer. Where we are,
There's daggers in men's smiles; the nea'er in blood,
The nearer bloody*.

the nea'er … bloody i.e. Duncan's closest relations, his sons, are most in danger of being the next murder victims

MALCOLM This murderous shaft that's shot
Hath not yet lighted, and our safest way
Is to avoid the aim. Therefore to horse,
And let us not be dainty of leave-taking,
But shift away. There's warrant in that theft
Which steals itself when there's no mercy left.
Exeunt

What do you think of the brothers' decision to leave the country?

Activities

A scene by 'Anonymous'?

Some critics have argued that the 'Porter scene' was not written by Shakespeare and should be left out of the play. Find arguments for and against this view.

1. Speculate on its dramatic function at this point (*comic relief).
2. Relate it to the 'serious' themes of the play, like damnation, illusion/delusion, authority, ambition, deceit, the gap between intention and action.

The actor Robert Armin, who played the Porter in 1607

'Porter of hell-gate.' From a 1976 Royal Shakespeare Company production

Take a look at Banquo's behaviour in this scene.

1. How does he react to the regicide?
2. What would you advise an actor playing Banquo to do while he isn't speaking?
3. Is there any indication that Banquo suspects the truth?

The silent witness

Establish a connection between the play's 'motto' – 'Fair is foul, and foul is fair' – and Macduff's statement in this scene that 'Confusion now hath made his masterpiece' (2.3.59).

The world turns topsy-turvy

Act 2 Scene 4

Some days later. It appears that the horror of the king's murder is mirrored by horrible and strange events in nature. The whole order of the world has been turned upside down. Macduff reports that Macbeth has been elected by the thanes to be the new king. He decides not to attend the coronation.

Enter ROSS, *with an* OLD MAN

OLD MAN Threescore* and ten I can remember well;
Within the volume of which time, I have seen
Hours dreadful and things strange, but this sore night
Hath trifled former knowings*.

ROSS Ha, good father,
Thou seest the heavens, as troubled with man's act,
Threatens his bloody stage. By th'clock 'tis day
And yet dark night strangles the travelling lamp*.
Is't night's predominance, or the day's shame,
That darkness does the face of earth entomb*
When living light should kiss it?

OLD MAN 'Tis unnatural,
Even like the deed* that's done. On Tuesday last,
A falcon tow'ring in her pride of place
Was by a mousing owl hawked at and killed.

ROSS And Duncan's horses, a thing most strange and certain,
Beauteous and swift, the minions of their race,
Turned wild in nature; broke their stalls, flung out,
Contending 'gainst obedience as* they would
Make war with mankind.

OLD MAN 'Tis said, they eat each other.

Threescore three times twenty (years)

trifled former knowings i.e. by comparison, my past experience seems trivial

lamp i.e. the sun

to entomb to bury

the deed i.e. the murder of the king

as as if

What meaning do the two men attribute to the strange events they have observed?

Scottish kings were traditionally crowned upon **the Stone of Scone** [sku:n]. Stolen by the English in 1296, it was returned to Scotland in 1996.

What … pretend? Why should they?
suborned paid
ravin up swallow greedily
like likely
Fife Macduff's home

The English coronation chair containing the Stone of Scone

ROSS They did so, to th'amazement of mine eyes
That looked upon't.

Enter MACDUFF

Here comes the good Macduff.
How goes the world, sir, now?

MACDUFF Why, see you not?

ROSS Is't known who did this more than bloody deed?

MACDUFF Those that Macbeth hath slain.

ROSS Alas the day,
What good could they pretend?*

MACDUFF They were suborned*.
Malcolm and Donaldbain, the king's two sons,
Are stol'n away and fled, which puts upon them
Suspicion of the deed.

ROSS 'Gainst nature still.
Thriftless ambition that will ravin up*
Thine own life's means. Then 'tis most like*
The sovereignty will fall upon Macbeth.

MACDUFF He is already named and gone to Scone
To be invested.

ROSS Where is Duncan's body?

MACDUFF Carried to Colmkill,
The sacred storehouse of his predecessors
And guardian of their bones.

ROSS Will you to Scone?

MACDUFF No, cousin, I'll to Fife*.

ROSS Well, I will thither.

MACDUFF Well may you see things well done there. Adieu,
Lest our old robes sit easier than our new.

ROSS Farewell, father.

OLD MAN God's benison go with you, and with those
That would make good of bad, and friends of foes.

Exeunt

Activities

A sceptic

1. Try to assess Macduff's manner and tone of voice. Be especially alert to hidden irony!
2. What is to be made of his decision to go home instead of attending Macbeth's coronation?

Reviewing Act Two

The king is dead

Take a look at the night of the king's assassination.

1. Make a film-script of 2.2 and 2.3: First, recount the on-stage *and* the off-stage events, then discuss the fact that some events are shown, others merely reported. Why, for instance, does Shakespeare prefer not to show the king's murder on stage? How does he create *tension and *suspense?
2. Would your film version of the night of the murder look different from Shakespeare's version?

Naturalizing the *status quo*

List all occurrences of the word 'nature' and its derivatives ('natural', 'unnatural', etc.) in act two. (It might help if you split yourselves into four groups, one for each scene.)

1. What ideas and values do the characters connect with the idea of 'nature'?
2. What do they mean when they call something or someone 'unnatural'?
3. What is the connection between the natural order and the political order?

The characters

After act one you were asked to assess the characters who had been introduced, and to describe their relationships with each other.

1. Does the characters' behaviour in act two correspond to your speculations about them?
2. Have their relationships developed in a way you could have foreseen?

A fly on a wall

The first three scenes of act two take place within one, certainly not more than two hours; during this time a king is murdered and his murderer makes a bid for the crown himself.

1. What is the atmosphere of the first three scenes of act two?
2. Identify and name Macbeth's and Lady Macbeth's strongest and most intense emotions during this time.
3. Imagine you were a fly on the Macbeths' bedroom wall: what did they do or talk about while they were waiting to be called out and pretend to be surprised by Macduff's and Lennox's arrival (i.e. the time between 2.2.77SD and 2.3.35SD)?

Act Three

Start here

Spirals of violence

'I am in
So far in blood that sin will pluck on sin:
Tear-falling pity dwells not in this eye.'
(*King Richard III,* 4.2.63-5)

'I am in blood
Stepped in so far that should I wade no more,
Returning were as tedious as go o'er.'
(*Macbeth,* 3.4.134-6)

These two famous Shakespearean villains claim that, in murdering their way to the top, they have reached a point of no return. Their past violence serves as a perverse kind of justification for more violence.

1. Paraphrase both quotations in your own words and point out the similarities and the differences between them.
2. Think of situations in which more violence seems necessary to make past violence worthwhile. Can you see the point of Richard's and Macbeth's arguments?

Adolf Hitler in World War II.

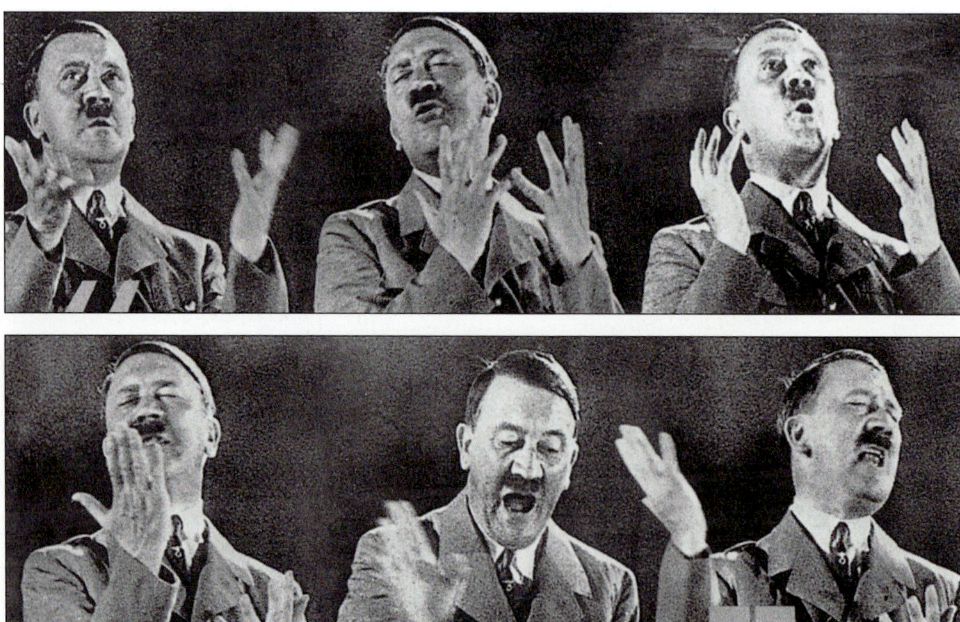

Act 3 Scene 1

One half of the Weird Sisters' prophecy has come true: Macbeth is king. Now he is tortured by the fear that the other half might become true as well: that the crown will go to Banquo's descendants. He hires two men to murder Banquo and his son, Fleance.

Enter BANQUO [*dressed for riding*]

BANQUO Thou hast it now, King, Cawdor, Glamis, all,
As the weird women promised, and I fear
Thou played'st most foully for't*; yet it was said
It should not stand in thy posterity*,
But that myself should be the root and father
Of many kings. If there come truth from them –
As upon thee, Macbeth, their speeches shine –
Why by the verities* on thee made good,
May they not be my oracles as well
And set me up in hope? But hush, no more.

Sennet sounded. Enter* MACBETH *as King,* LADY [MACBETH *as Queen*], LENNOX, ROSS, *Lords, and Attendants*

MACBETH Here's our chief guest.

LADY MACBETH If he had been forgotten,
It had been as a gap in our great feast
And all thing unbecoming*.

played'st ... for't got the crown by criminal means
stand ... posterity go down to your children
verities truths

≺ Does Banquo interrupt himself, or is he interrupted by the entering group of people?

Val: Look, he is king now. I think he looks a bit uncomfortable, with his crown and gown, don't you?

Sennet trumpet call
all thing unbecoming absolutely inappropriate

Shakespeare read about the reign of King Macbeth of Scotland (1040-57) in **Elizabethan *chronicles**, whose depiction of events differs in some significant points from the story Shakespeare tells in the play. For instance, in the chronicles Banquo is Macbeth's willing accomplice – you will see whether this is true in the play!

'Thou hast it now.' From Polanski's film (1971)

MACBETH Tonight we hold a solemn supper, sir,
And I'll request your presence.

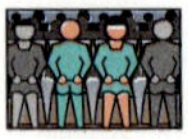

Ian: Do you hear an undertone in Banquo's reply?

BANQUO Let your highness
Command upon me, to the which my duties
Are with a most indissoluble tie
Forever knit.

Why is Macbeth so interested in Banquo's leisure activities?

MACBETH Ride you this afternoon?

BANQUO Ay, my good lord.

MACBETH We should have else desired your good advice
Which still hath been both grave and prosperous
In this day's council: but we'll take tomorrow*.
Is't far you ride?

we'll take tomorrow we'll wait till tomorrow (to discuss state matters)

BANQUO As far, my lord, as will fill up the time
'Twixt this and supper. Go not my horse the better,
I must become a borrower of the night
For a dark hour, or twain*.

Go not … twain If my horse isn't fast enough, I'll be an hour or two late (for supper).

MACBETH Fail not our feast.

BANQUO My lord, I will not.

MACBETH We hear our bloody cousins are bestowed
In England and in Ireland, not confessing
Their cruel parricide*, filling their hearers
With strange invention. But of that tomorrow,
When therewithal we shall have cause of state
Craving us jointly*. Hie you to horse; adieu,
Till you return at night. Goes Fleance with you?

parricide murder of a father by his child

To whom is Macbeth speaking these official-sounding lines? To Banquo or to the courtiers?

Craving us jointly Requiring us both

BANQUO Ay, my good lord; our time does call upon's.

MACBETH I wish your horses swift and sure of foot,
And so I do commend you to their backs.
Farewell.

Exit Banquo

Let every man be master of his time
Till seven at night; to make society
The sweeter welcome, we will keep ourself
Till supper-time alone. While then, God be with you.

Exeunt [all but Macbeth and a Servant]

Sirrah*, a word with you: attend those men
Our pleasure?

Sirrah (form of address to a social inferior)

SERVANT They are, my lord, without the palace gate.

MACBETH Bring them before us.

Exit Servant

What does Macbeth mean by 'thus'?

To be thus is nothing,
But to be safely thus. Our fears in Banquo
Stick deep, and in his royalty of nature
Reigns that which would be feared. 'Tis much he dares,
And to that dauntless temper of his mind,

He hath a wisdom that doth guide his valour
To act in safety. There is none but he,
Whose being I do fear; and under him
My genius is rebuked*, as it is said
Mark Antony's was by Caesar. He chid* the sisters
When first they put the name of king upon me
And bade them speak to him. Then prophet-like,
They hailed him father to a line of kings.
Upon my head they placed a fruitless crown
And put a barren sceptre in my gripe,
Thence to be wrenched with an unlineal hand*,
No son of mine succeeding. If't be so,
For Banquo's issue* have I filed* my mind;
For them, the gracious Duncan have I murdered,
Put rancours in the vessel of my peace
Only for them, and mine eternal jewel
Given to the common enemy of man,
To make them kings, the seeds of Banquo kings.
Rather than so, come Fate into the list*,
And champion me to th'utterance*. Who's there?

Enter Servant and two MURDERERS

[*To Servant*] Now go to the door and stay there till we call.
Exit Servant

Was it not yesterday we spoke together?

MURDERERS It was, so please your highness.

MACBETH Well then, now have you considered of my speeches? Know, that it was he in the times past which held you so un-

under him ... rebuked my guiding spirit (guardian angel) is conquered by Banquo
chid chided, rebuked
Thence ... hand To be taken from me violently and by someone unrelated to me by blood

Ian: 'If't be so'? That's what the witches told him straight away. There's no need to be surprised now!

What is his 'eternal jewel', and who is the 'common enemy of man' to whom he has given it?

issue children, descendants
filed defiled, made dirty
list tournament area where knights fight with lances and swords
th'utterance the utmost, i.e. death

Seeing the play on stage, at which point in the ensuing dialogue would you realize that the two men are hired killers?

'... have you considered of my speeches?' From Orson Welles' film (1948)

made good proved beyond doubt
borne in hand deceived, misled with false promises
notion mind

Are … gospelled Do you believe so firmly in the biblical command to love your enemy?
beggared yours has reduced your family to poverty

clept called
valued file list in which things are arranged by value and quality

closed enclosed (i.e. which nature has given him)
whereby … alike which sets him apart, by some special quality, from the average

Val: Wait a moment, this 'Are-you-a-man-or-a-mouse'-strategy sounds very familiar!
Ian: Yes, and now he is using it on someone else. Well, he should know how much it hurts!

Grapples Hooks, fastens tightly
in his life while he is alive

tugged with knocked around by

distance enmity, hatred
near'st of life heart (The metaphor in these lines is taken from fencing.)

What would be the opposite ➤ of 'barefaced'?

der fortune, which you thought had been our innocent self. This I made good* to you in our last conference; passed in probation with you how you were borne in hand*, how crossed; the instruments, who wrought with them, and all things else that might to half a soul and to a notion* crazed say, 'Thus did Banquo.'

First Murderer You made it known to us.

Macbeth I did so, and went further, which is now our point of second meeting. Do you find your patience so predominant in your nature, that you can let this go? Are you so gospelled*, to pray for this good man and for his issue, whose heavy hand hath bowed you to the grave and beggared yours* forever?

First Murderer We are men, my liege.

Macbeth Ay, in the catalogue ye go for men,
As hounds, and greyhounds, mongrels, spaniels, curs,
Shoughs, water-rugs, and demi-wolves are clept*
All by the name of dogs. The valued file*
Distinguishes the swift, the slow, the subtle,
The housekeeper, the hunter, every one
According to the gift which bounteous nature
Hath in him closed*, whereby he does receive
Particular addition from the bill
That writes them all alike*. And so of men.
Now, if you have a station in the file
Not i'th'worst rank of manhood, say't,
And I will put that business in your bosoms,
Whose execution takes your enemy off,
Grapples* you to the heart and love of us
Who wear our health but sickly in his life*,
Which in his death were perfect.

Second Murderer I am one, my liege,
Whom the vile blows and buffets of the world
Hath so incensed that I am reckless what I do
To spite the world.

First Murderer And I another,
So weary with disasters, tugged with* fortune,
That I would set my life on any chance
To mend it or be rid on't.

Macbeth Both of you know
Banquo was your enemy.

Murderers True, my lord.

Macbeth So is he mine, and in such bloody distance*
That every minute of his being thrusts
Against my near'st of life*, and though I could
With barefaced power sweep him from my sight

And bid my will avouch it*, yet I must not,
For certain friends that are both his and mine,
Whose loves I may not drop, but wail his fall
Who I myself struck down. And thence it is
That I to your assistance do make love*,
Masking the business from the common eye
For sundry weighty reasons.

SECOND MURDERER We shall, my lord,
Perform what you command us.

FIRST MURDERER Though our lives –

MACBETH Your spirits shine through you. Within this hour at most,
I will advise you where to plant yourselves,
Acquaint you with the perfect spy o'th'time*,
The moment on't, for't must be done tonight,
And something from* the palace: always thought,
That I require a clearness*. And with him,
To leave no rubs nor botches in the work,
Fleance, his son that keeps him company,
Whose absence is no less material to me
Than is his father's, must embrace the fate
Of that dark hour. Resolve yourselves apart,
I'll come to you anon*.

MURDERERS We are resolved, my lord.

MACBETH I'll call upon you straight; abide within.
[*Exeunt Murderers*]
It is concluded. Banquo, thy soul's flight,
If it find heaven, must find it out tonight. *Exit*

though … avouch it though, as an absolute ruler, I could simply kill him and 'justify' myself by saying it was my wish

That I … love That I flatter you by asking your assistance

perfect spy o'th'time (The meaning is obscure: it may mean a third murderer (cf. 3.3) or, more probably, 'the best way to go about it'.)
something from a certain distance away from
I … clearness I must seem unconnected to the deed.

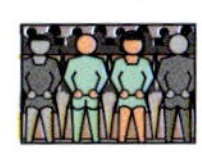
Val: 'Embrace the fate / Of that dark hour'? The coward, why doesn't he spell it out?

anon at once

Activities

3.1.1–10 is Banquo's only *soliloquy in the whole play and the only time he comments on the events he has witnessed.

1. He addresses Macbeth as if he were present (apostrophe). What does this say about Banquo's state of mind? What is the dramatic effect?
2. What does he think about Macbeth's coronation? What about the prophecy?
3. Where does he see himself in all this? Can you detect any moral judgement in his words? It is clear that he *knows*, but what does he intend to *do*?

'Silence is consent'?

Delegating a murder ➤

The murder of Banquo is not unproblematic. Macbeth has to 'mask the business from the common eye' (124) because he 'require[s] a clearness' (132). He wants killers to do the job for him and proceeds with great care to manipulate them and to prepare them for it.

1. Make a list of the opinions and feelings Macbeth has to evoke in the Murderers. Cite passages from the text and paraphrase them in your own words.
2. Then list the arguments and rhetorical strategies by which he manipulates them.
   By the way: is there any mention of money or payment in this transaction?

Act 3 Scene 2

Husband and wife exchange their worries and fears about their precarious situation. Lady Macbeth tries to calm him down, but Macbeth feels sure that only more violence will bring security. He hints at another murder but won't tell his wife what he has in mind.

Enter [LADY MACBETH] *and a* SERVANT

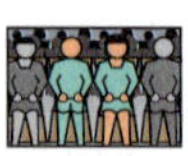

Ian: What 's happening? She never used to be so formal with him!

LADY MACBETH Is Banquo gone from court?

SERVANT Ay, madam, but returns again tonight.

LADY MACBETH Say to the king, I would attend his leisure
For a few words.

SERVANT Madam I will. *Exit*

Nought Nothing
spent lost

LADY MACBETH Nought's* had, all's spent*
Where our desire is got without content.
'Tis safer to be that which we destroy
Than by destruction dwell in doubtful joy.

Enter MACBETH

sorriest fancies most dreadful fantasies
scorched slashed, stabbed
to close to rejoin, heal
poor malice weak, small crimes

How now, my lord, why do you keep alone
Of sorriest fancies* your companions making,
Using those thoughts which should indeed have died
With them they think on? Things without all remedy
Should be without regard; what's done, is done.

The actor has to decide ➤ whether 'we' and 'us' means Macbeth as king or the Macbeths as a couple. How would you play it?

MACBETH We have scorched* the snake, not killed it;
She'll close*, and be herself, whilst our poor malice*
Remains in danger of her former tooth.

'… terrible dreams … shake us nightly'. Laurence Olivier and Vivien Leigh in a 1955 London theatre production

But let the frame of things disjoint*, both the worlds*
  suffer,
Ere we will eat our meal in fear and sleep
In the affliction of these terrible dreams
That shake us nightly. Better be with the dead
Whom we, to gain our peace, have sent to peace,
Than on the torture of the mind to lie
In restless ecstasy*. Duncan is in his grave.
After life's fitful fever, he sleeps well;
Treason has done his worst; nor steel nor* poison,
Malice domestic, foreign levy, nothing
Can touch him further.

LADY MACBETH Come on. Gentle my lord,
Sleek o'er* your rugged looks, be bright and jovial
Among your guests tonight.

MACBETH So shall I, love,
And so I pray be you. Let your remembrance
Apply to Banquo, present him eminence*
Both with eye and tongue; unsafe the while, that we
Must lave our honours in these flattering streams*
And make our faces vizards* to our hearts,
Disguising what they are.

LADY MACBETH You must leave this.

MACBETH O, full of scorpions is my mind, dear wife!
Thou know'st that Banquo and his Fleance lives.

LADY MACBETH But in them Nature's copy's not eterne*.

let … disjoint let the world fall to pieces
both the worlds this world and the next

ecstasy a state of being beside oneself (here, with fear and guilt)
nor … nor neither … nor (common Elizabethan usage)

A Macbeth sees many advantages in being dead. What are they?

Sleek o'er Smooth over

present him eminence pay him particular respect
unsafe … streams as long as we are unsafe, we have to clean our titles (i.e. king and queen) in the waters of flattery
vizards masks

But … eterne Their lives are not eternal.

jocund cheerful
ere before
Hecate ['hekət] goddess of witchcraft

MACBETH There's comfort yet, they are assailable;
Then be thou jocund*: ere* the bat hath flown
His cloistered flight, ere to black Hecate's* summons
The shard-borne beetle with his drowsy hums
Hath rung night's yawning peal, there shall be done
A deed of dreadful note.

LADY MACBETH What's to be done?

chuck chicken (a term of affection)
seeling blinding (as with a scarf about the eyes)
pitiful full of pity

that great ... pale the law of life, the commandment against murder, which protects Banquo because Macbeth feels daunted ('pale') by it
night's black agents animals active by night (but with an allusion to evil spirits)
hold thee still remain calm

MACBETH Be innocent of the knowledge, dearest chuck*,
Till thou applaud the deed. Come, seeling* night,
Scarf up the tender eye of pitiful* day
And with thy bloody and invisible hand
Cancel and tear to pieces that great bond
Which keeps me pale*. Light thickens,
And the crow makes wing to th'rooky wood;
Good things of day begin to droop and drowse,
Whiles night's black agents* to their preys do rouse.
Thou marvell'st at my words, but hold thee still*;
Things bad begun, make strong themselves by ill.
So prithee, go with me.

Exeunt

Activities

Antithesis and structure

A very successful director of Shakespeare's plays once said:

> 'If I were to offer one single bit of advice to an actor new to Shakespeare's text, [I would say,] 'Look for the antitheses and play them'.'
>
> (John Barton, *Playing Shakespeare*, Methuen, London, 1984, p. 55).

In this scene, both the Macbeths are torn between what they have achieved and what they had wished for. Reread the scene closely and look for the *antitheses which express their feeling of 'Nought's had, all's spent'.

Note that antithetical terms need not come up in the same line, but can be scattered over several lines.

Present a dumb show

Working in pairs, stage the exchange between husband and wife in a *dumb show. Pay particular attention to their movements and decide at which points the couple should be physically close to each other and at which they should be moving apart. Don't be afraid to be stylized, and don't hesitate to touch, should the words seem to call for it.

You might be surprised how much of the dramatic impact of the scene can be conveyed merely by the movements of the actors!

Act 3 Scene 3

Banquo and Fleance are waylaid on their return to the castle. Banquo is murdered, but Fleance escapes.

Enter three MURDERERS

FIRST MURDERER But who did bid thee join with us?

THIRD MURDERER Macbeth.

SECOND MURDERER He* needs not our mistrust, since he delivers
Our offices* and what we have to do
To the direction just*.

FIRST MURDERER [*To Third Murderer*] Then stand with us.
The west yet glimmers with some streaks of day;
Now spurs the lated traveller apace
To gain the timely* inn and near approaches
The subject of our watch*.

THIRD MURDERER Hark, I hear horses.

BANQUO (*within**) Give us a light there, ho!

SECOND MURDERER Then 'tis he; the rest
That are within the note of expectation
Already are i'th'court.

FIRST MURDERER His horses go about.

THIRD MURDERER Almost a mile; but he does usually,
So all men do, from hence to th'palace gate
Make it their walk.

Enter BANQUO *and* FLEANCE, *with a torch*

SECOND MURDERER A light, a light!

THIRD MURDERER 'Tis he.

FIRST MURDERER Stand to't.

BANQUO It will be rain tonight.

FIRST MURDERER Let it come down.
[*The Murderers attack. First Murderer strikes out the light*]

BANQUO O, treachery!
Fly, good Fleance, fly, fly, fly!
Thou mayst revenge – O slave! [*Dies. Fleance escapes*]

THIRD MURDERER Who did strike out the light?

FIRST MURDERER Was't not the way*?

THIRD MURDERER There's but one down; the son is fled.

Implicit *stage directions: The first sentence of the scene does not sound like the first sentence of a conversation. The actors are supposed to enter the stage in the *middle* of a heated exchange, which means that the scene has the necessary speed and energy right from the start.

He i.e. Third Murderer

offices tasks

To … just Exactly, precisely

timely coming up at the right moment at the end of a day's journey

The subject … watch The man we are waiting for, i.e. Banquo

within (Banquo is not supposed to be inside a building; he is calling from behind the stage to give the illusion of distance.)

≺ How and why does Shakespeare get rid of Banquo's and Fleance's horses before the two men enter the scene?

≺ What is the grim double meaning of 'it' in the First Murderer's cry of attack?

the way the right way to go about the murder

SECOND MURDERER We have lost best half of our affair.

FIRST MURDERER Well, let's away, and say how much is done.
Exeunt [*with Banquo's body*]

'Let it come down.' From Polanski's film (1971)

Activities

Staging a murder

Talk about the difficulties in staging this scene: it is set outside and in the dark, lit only by the flame of a torch. Also, it is very short and full of violent action.

1. What could the actors and a director do in order to clarify the events for the audience?
2. What solutions to these staging problems would you suggest for a theatre production, which for a film?

Act 3 Scene 4

The Macbeths have invited the Scottish aristocracy to a big state banquet. Macbeth's attention is distracted: first by the message that Fleance has escaped his killers, then by an appearance of Banquo's Ghost, which scares him so much that he betrays himself in front of his guests. Lady Macbeth fails to save the situation; the banquet is broken off.

A sensitive killer

So far we have come to know Macbeth as an extremely sensitive murderer, haunted by terrible visions whenever he thinks of his victims.

1. Look for such passages in acts one and two.
2. How do you expect him to react when he learns about the cruel slaughter of his latest victim?

Banquet prepared: Two thrones are placed on stage.
Enter MACBETH [*as King*] LADY [*MACBETH as Queen*], ROSS, LENNOX, LORDS, *and Attendants. Lady Macbeth sits*

MACBETH You know your own degrees*, sit down;
[*The Lords sit*]
at first and last, the hearty welcome.

degrees titles, rank (important for the seating order)

LORDS Thanks to your majesty.

MACBETH Our self will mingle with society and play the humble host; our hostess keeps her state, but in best time we will require her welcome.

LADY MACBETH Pronounce it for me, sir, to all our friends for my heart speaks, they are welcome.

Enter FIRST MURDERER

MACBETH See, they encounter thee with their hearts' thanks.
Both sides are even; here I'll sit i'th'midst.
Be large in mirth, anon we'll drink a measure
The table round. [*To First Murderer*] There's blood upon thy face.

FIRST MURDERER 'Tis Banquo's then.

MACBETH 'Tis better thee without, than he within.
Is he dispatched*?

dispatched sent off, i.e. killed

FIRST MURDERER My lord, his throat is cut; that I did for him.

the like the same
the nonpareil the best

MACBETH Thou art the best o'th'cut-throats,
Yet he's good that did the like* for Fleance;
If thou didst it, thou art the nonpareil*.

FIRST MURDERER Most royal sir, Fleance is scaped.

fit a sudden attack of fear
casing surrounding
cabined, cribbed, confined shut into a very small space, like an animal

MACBETH Then comes my fit* again: I had else been perfect;
Whole as the marble, founded as the rock,
As broad and general as the casing* air:
But now I am cabined, cribbed, confined*, bound in
To saucy doubts and fears. But Banquo's safe?

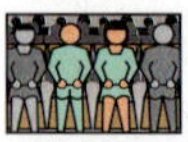
Ian: 'Banquo's safe?' Now, that really is a sick *pun!
Val: Well, foul is fair … remember?

FIRST MURDERER Ay, my good lord: safe in a ditch he bides,
With twenty trenchèd gashes on his head,
The least a death to nature.

worm the baby snake, i.e. Fleance

MACBETH Thanks for that.
There the grown serpent lies; the worm* that's fled
Hath nature that in time will venom breed,
No teeth for th'present. Get thee gone; tomorrow
We'll hear ourselves again. *Exit [First] Murderer*

You … cheer You do not propose the toast everyone is waiting for. (Lady Macbeth is encouraging her husband to be more attentive to their guests.)

LADY MACBETH My royal lord,
You do not give the cheer*; the feast is sold
That is not often vouched while 'tis a-making
'Tis given with welcome. To feed were best at home:
From thence, the sauce to meat is ceremony,
Meeting were bare without it.

***Onomatopoeia**
[ˌɒnəˌmætəˈpiːə]: Note how the size of the stab wounds in Banquo's head is aurally stressed by the word 'trenchèd' being pronounced with two syllables.

Enter the GHOST OF BANQUO *and sits in Macbeth's place*

MACBETH Sweet remembrancer!
Now good digestion wait on appetite,
And health on both.

LENNOX May't please your highness, sit.

our country's honour all of Scotland's noblemen

Who … mischance I hope it is only impoliteness ('unkindness') that has kept him away, not an accident.

MACBETH Here had we now our country's honour* roofed,
Were the graced person of our Banquo present,
Who may I rather challenge for unkindness
Than pity for mischance*.

ROSS His absence, sir,
Lays blame upon his promise. Please't your highness
To grace us with your royal company?

MACBETH The table's full.

LENNOX Here is a place reserved, sir.

MACBETH Where?

LENNOX Here, my good lord. What is't that moves your highness?

What does Macbeth see? ➤

MACBETH Which of you have done this?

LORDS What, my good lord?

'Which of you have done this?' Set design for a Victorian theatre production (1853)

MACBETH Thou canst not say I did it; never shake
Thy gory* locks at me!

ROSS Gentlemen, rise, his highness is not well.

[*Lady Macbeth joins the Lords*]

LADY MACBETH Sit, worthy friends. My lord is often thus,
And hath been from his youth. Pray you, keep seat.
The fit is momentary; upon a thought
He will again be well. If much you note* him
You shall offend him and extend his passion.
Feed, and regard him not. [*To Macbeth*] Are you a man?

MACBETH Ay, and a bold* one, that dare look on that
Which might appal the devil.

LADY MACBETH O proper stuff*!
This is thc very painting of your fear;
This is the air-drawn dagger which you said
Led you to Duncan. O, these flaws and starts*,
Impostors to true fear, would well become*

gory covered in blood

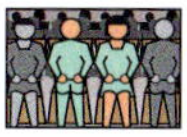

Ian: Oh no, not *that* again! Must she go on and on about his dratted manhood?
Val: Seems to be a sore point with them …

to note to give attention to

bold brave, daring

proper stuff complete nonsense

flaws and starts physical signs of hysteria

to become to suit

grandam grandmother

A woman's story at a winter's fire
Authorised by her grandam*. Shame itself!
Why do you make such faces? When all's done
You look but on a stool.

monuments tombs, graves
our … kites we shall find rest only in the stomachs of birds who eat our dead bodies

MACBETH Prithee, see there! Behold, look, lo! How say you?
[*To Ghost*] Why, what care I? If thou canst nod, speak too.
If charnel houses and our graves must send
Those that we bury back, our monuments*
Shall be the maws of kites*.

[*Exit Ghost of Banquo*]

LADY MACBETH What, quite unmanned in folly?

MACBETH If I stand here, I saw him.

LADY MACBETH Fie, for shame.

Ere … weal Before humans designed laws to prevent violence in society
The time has been There was a time

What else might Macbeth be thinking of when he says 'crowns' and 'stools'?

MACBETH Blood hath been shed ere now, i'th'olden time,
Ere humane statute purged the gentle weal*;
Ay, and since too, murders have been performed
Too terrible for the ear. The time has been*
That when the brains were out, the man would die,
And there an end. But now they rise again
With twenty mortal murders on their crowns
And push us from our stools. This is more strange
Than such a murder is.

LADY MACBETH My worthy lord,
Your noble friends do lack you.

to muse to wonder
infirmity weakness

MACBETH I do forget –
Do not muse* at me, my most worthy friends.
I have a strange infirmity* which is nothing
To those that know me. Come, love and health to all,
Then I'll sit down. Give me some wine; fill full!

Enter GHOST [OF BANQUO]

Comment on the ironic juxtaposition of the *stage direction and Macbeth's words.

I drink to th'general joy o'th'whole table,
And to our dear friend Banquo, whom we miss.
Would he were here! To all, and him we thirst,
And all to all.

LORDS Our duties and the pledge.

Avaunt Away with you
speculation ability to see

MACBETH Avaunt* and quit my sight! Let the earth hide thee!
Thy bones are marrowless, thy blood is cold
Thou hast no speculation* in those eyes
Which thou dost glare with.

LADY MACBETH Think of this, good peers,
But as a thing of custom. 'Tis no other,
only it spoils the pleasure of the time.

MACBETH What man dare, I dare;
Approach thou like the rugged Russian bear,

'… armed rhinoceros.' From an Elizabethan engraving

The armed rhinoceros, or th'Hyrcan tiger,
Take any shape but that*, and my firm nerves
Shall never tremble. Or be alive again,
And dare me to the desert with thy sword;
If trembling I inhabit then, protest me*
The baby of a girl*. Hence horrible shadow,
Unreal mock'ry* hence.

[*Exit Ghost of Banquo*]

Why so, being gone,
I am a man again. – Pray you, sit still.

LADY MACBETH You have displaced the mirth*, broke the good meeting
With most admired* disorder.

MACBETH Can such things be,
And overcome us like a summer's cloud,
Without our special wonder? You make me strange
Even to the disposition that I owe*,
When now I think you can behold such sights
And keep the natural ruby of your cheeks,
When mine is blanched* with fear.

ROSS What sights, my lord?

LADY MACBETH I pray you speak not; he grows worse and worse.
Question enrages him. At once, good night.
Stand not upon the order of your going,
But go at once.

LENNOX Good night, and better health
Attend his majesty.

LADY MACBETH A kind good night to all.

[*Exeunt*] *Lords* [*and Attendants*]

but that i.e. Banquo's spirit could appear in any horrible form, it wouldn't frighten Macbeth as much as the sight of Banquo as he looked when he was murdered
protest me publicly call me
baby of a girl a girl's doll
mock'ry mockery (i.e. an imitation of something, intended to mock and ridicule)

mirth cheerfulness

admired surprising, alarming (The word didn't have today's connotation of 'inspiring respect'.)

You … owe Your coolness makes me appear unfamiliar even to myself.

blanched pale

➤ How do you picture the departure of the guests?

MACBETH It will have blood they say: blood will have blood.
Stones have been known to move and trees to speak.
Augures*, and understood relations*, have
By maggot-pies, and choughs*, and rooks brought forth
The secret'st man of blood*. What is the night?

LADY MACBETH Almost at odds with morning, which is which*.

MACBETH How sayst thou that Macduff denies his person
At our great bidding*?

LADY MACBETH Did you send to him, sir?

MACBETH I hear it by the way, but I will send.
There's not a one of them* but in his house
I keep a servant feed*. I will tomorrow –
And betimes I will – to the weird sisters.
More shall they speak. For now I am bent to know
By the worst means, the worst; for mine own good,
All causes shall give way. I am in blood
Stepped in so far that should I wade* no more,
Returning were as tedious as go o'er.
Strange things I have in head that will to hand,
Which must be acted ere they may be scanned*.

LADY MACBETH You lack the season of all natures, sleep.

MACBETH Come, we'll to sleep. My strange and self-abuse
Is the initiate fear that wants hard use*;
We are yet but young in deed.

Exeunt

Augures Omens
relations predictions
maggot-pies, and choughs magpies and crows (who were thought to be able to speak)
The secret'st ... blood The most secretive, careful murderer
Almost ... which It's not clear whether it's night or day.
How ... bidding What do you say to the fact that Macduff didn't follow our royal invitation?
them the Scottish noblemen
feed paid (i.e. to spy for me)

to wade to walk through water (or, as here, through blood)
scanned thought about
My ... use It isn't like me to become hysterical – more practice (i.e. in killing) will dispel these beginner's weaknesses.

Ian: Oh, heck, that sounds ominous! Like in the movies: 'You ain't seen nothin' yet, Babe ...!'

Activities

A party goes to pieces

The 'banquet scene' starts in an atmosphere of ceremony and ordered conviviality, and gradually degenerates into complete chaos, panic and embarrassment.

1. Describe the development from order to disorder: what are the events that cause it?
2. How do the hosts and their guests deal with the extremely awkward situation?

Keywords

There are various keywords in this scene which occur several times, e.g. 'fear', 'blood', 'man', 'strange', 'order' and 'sleep'. Choose two such words and write an essay on their significance in this scene. When and where necessary, refer to the play so far as you know it.

An eyewitness reports

On 20 April 1611, the physician and astrologer Simon Forman made a note in his diary about a performance of *Macbeth* he had seen shortly before:

> 'The next night, being at supper with his noble men whom he had bid to a feaste to the which also Banco should have come, he began to speak of the Noble Banco, and to wish that he wer there. And as he thus did, standing up to drincke a Carouse [ie. a toast] to him, the ghoste of Banco came and sate down in his cheier behind him. And he turninge about to sit down Again sawe the goste of Banco, which feared [i.e. frightened] him so, that he fell in a great passion of fear and fury …'

1. Modernize the spelling of this quotation, and give the lines of the passage Forman is describing.
2. What can you infer from this account about the presentation of the Ghost and its movement on the stage? For instance, at which point does the Ghost enter?
3. Can you tell what stage effects or speeches have impressed Forman most strongly?

Act 3 Scene 5

Hecate, goddess of witchcraft, scolds the Weird Sisters for their dealings with Macbeth. She knows that he will come to see them again soon, and orders them to prepare themselves.

Thunder. Enter the three WITCHES, *meeting* HECATE

FIRST WITCH Why how now, Hecate, you look angerly*?

HECATE Have I not reason, beldams*, as you are,
Saucy* and over-bold? How did you dare
To trade and traffic* with Macbeth
In riddles and affairs of death?
And I the mistress of your charms*,
The close contriver* of all harms,
Was never called to bear my part
Or show the glory of our art*?
And which is worse, all you have done
Hath been but for a wayward* son,

angerly angrily

beldams ugly old women
saucy naughty, irreverent
trade and traffic have dealings with

charms magic spells
close contriver of secret force behind

our art i.e. witchcraft

wayward wild, uncontrollable

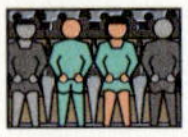

Ian: Did you hear that? They called Macbeth their 'weird son' – he's one of them now!
Val: 'Wayward', actually, not 'weird'.
Ian: So? Ever heard of aural *puns?

Acheron ['ækərɒn] river in hell (in Greek mythology)

vap'rous drop profound watery substance with magic qualities
sleights tricks
artificial artful, full of clever deceit
sprites spirits, apparitions

security over-confidence

Elizabethan stage effects: When *Macbeth* was performed at the Globe in 1607, Hecate vanished by being pulled up to the 'foggy cloud' and through an opening in the roof of the stage.

Spiteful and wrathful, who, as others do,
Loves for his own ends, not for you.
But make amends now. Get you gone,
And at the pit of Acheron*
Meet me i'th'morning. Thither he
Will come to know his destiny.
Your vessels and your spells provide,
Your charms and every thing beside.
I am for th'air. This night I'll spend
Unto a dismal and a fatal end.
Great business must be wrought ere noon.
Upon the corner of the moon
There hangs a vap'rous drop profound*;
I'll catch it ere it come to ground;
And that distilled by magic sleights*,
Shall raise such artificial* sprites*
As by the strength of their illusion
Shall draw him on to his confusion.
He shall spurn fate, scorn death, and bear
His hopes 'bove wisdom, grace, and fear.
And you all know, security*
Is mortals' chiefest enemy.

Music, and a song [*'Come away, come away', within*]
Hark, I am called: my little spirit, see,
Sits in a foggy cloud, and stays for me. [*Exit*]

FIRST WITCH Come, let's make haste; she'll soon be back again.

Exeunt

Activities

Another scene by 'Anonymous'?

Critics have been discussing for quite a while whether this scene was written by Shakespeare or by some other Elizabethan playwright.

1. Why would it be interesting or important to know which parts of a play or a novel were not written by the main author? Does it matter at all?
2. What would be missing if the 'Hecate scene' were cut in a production of *Macbeth?*
3. What is gained by including it?

Act 3 Scene 6

Very guardedly at first, then more openly, two Scottish lords exchange their opinions and feelings about Macbeth's misrule of the country. Their good wishes are with Malcolm, Duncan's son, who is staying at the English court, and with Macduff, who still refuses to attend Macbeth.

Enter LENNOX *and another* LORD

LENNOX My former speeches have but hit your thoughts
Which can interpret further*; only I say
Things have been strangely borne*. The gracious Duncan
Was pitied of Macbeth; marry*, he was dead.
And the right-valiant Banquo walked too late*,
Whom you may say, if't please you, Fleance killed,
For Fleance fled. Men must not walk too late.
Who cannot want the thought* how monstrous
It was for Malcolm and for Donaldbain
To kill their gracious father? Damnèd fact,
How it did grieve Macbeth! Did he not straight
In pious rage the two delinquents tear,
That were the slaves of drink and thralls of sleep?
Was not that nobly done? Ay, and wisely too,
For 'twould have angered any heart alive
To hear the men deny't. So that I say,
He has borne all things well, and I do think
That had he Duncan's sons under his key* –
As, an't* please heaven, he shall not – they should find
What 'twere to kill a father. So should Fleance.
But peace*, for from broad words* and 'cause he failed
His presence at the tyrant's feast, I hear
Macduff lives in disgrace. Sir, can you tell
Where he bestows himself*?

LORD The son of Duncan*,
From whom this tyrant holds the due of birth*,
Lives in the English court and is received
Of the most pious Edward* with such grace,
That the malevolence of fortune nothing
Takes from his high respect. Thither Macduff
Is gone to pray the holy king upon his aid*
To wake Northumberland and warlike Siward
That by the help of these, with him above*
To ratify the work, we may again
Give to our tables meat, sleep to our nights,
Free from our feasts and banquets bloody knives,
Do faithful homage and receive free honours,

My … further What I have said so far is only what you were thinking yourself, and you can guess the implications, which I am leaving unsaid.
borne carried out, managed
marry by the virgin Mary (a mild oath)
walked too late was out late at night (which is always dangerous)
Who … thought Who can help thinking

Val: Boy, when I read this speech at school, I didn't realize how *sarcastic* Lennox is!

under his key imprisoned
an't if it

But peace But I'll be quiet now
broad words critical remarks

bestows himself is staying

son of Duncan i.e. Malcolm
holds … birth keeps what he has inherited, i.e. the crown

pious Edward King Edward the Confessor (died 1066)

to pray … aid to beg Edward to help him

him above God

pine wish
exasperate made furious
their king i.e. the English king
he i.e. Macbeth (The use of pronouns is confusing here. It makes sense to assume that Macbeth looms so large in the two men's minds that they know immediately who is meant by 'he' here, even though one line before 'he' meant King Edward.)
turns me turns ('me' is only added for emphasis; the Lord was not the messenger.)
You'll … answer You'll regret having given me such an insulting answer (The messenger knows that Macduff will be in trouble.)

Why do the two men advise Macduff to stay away from Macbeth?

Advise … provide If he knows what's good for him, Macduff will keep away from Macbeth.

All which we pine* for now. And this report
Hath so exasperate* their king* that he
Prepares for some attempt of war.

LENNOX Sent he* to Macduff?

LORD He did. And with an absolute, 'Sir, not I',
The cloudy messenger turns me* his back
And hums, as who should say, 'You'll rue the time
That clogs me with this answer*'.

LENNOX And that well might
Advise him to a caution t'hold what distance
His wisdom can provide.* Some holy angel
Fly to the court of England and unfold
His message ere he come, that a swift blessing
May soon return to this our suffering country
Under a hand accursed.

LORD I'll send my prayers with him.

Exeunt

Activities

Murmuring subjects

'Irony is a technique of saying as little and meaning as much as possible.'
Look at Lennox's first speech in this scene, and apply the above statement to it.

1. Read out sentences in which he seems to be meaning more than he says. How does he indicate to the Lord that there is something he is not saying outright?
2. What do you imagine his manner and tone of voice to be like? Do they change in the course of his speech? If so, at which points?
3. What is the most outspoken (and, thus, dangerous) thing Lennox says in order to find out the Lord's opinions about Macbeth?
4. Why does Lennox have to disguise his thoughts at all? Why does he have to use irony and other *rhetorical tricks to say what he thinks?

Reviewing Act Three

A tête-à-tête

Work in pairs with Macbeth's soliloquy (3.1.49–73): Sitting face to face and knee to knee, one person reads out the speech to his or her partner, substituting 'you there' for 'Banquo', 'you' for 'he', etc. 'Macbeth' should try as hard as possible to communicate his or her thoughts and emotions to 'Banquo'. Read as slowly as necessary, and repeat the words, clauses or sentences that seem especially important to you. Read it through several times, then change roles.
How does the speech make you feel?
Which thought or emotion is predominant in it?

Enter a ghost

What do you think of some directors' decision to have a Ghost that is visible *only* to Macbeth and not to the theatre audience? What does this decision mean for the audience?

1. As a class, discuss how you would stage the appearances of the Ghost. If you read the text very carefully, you will find many directions by Shakespeare to the actors about how to act and what to do. Remember to bear in mind that the Ghost and Macbeth are not the only people on stage! Be as specific as you can about the set and the looks, actions and reactions of every character or group of characters.
2. Then act it.

'You look but on a stool.' From a BBC film (1982)

Born to be a murderer?

Considering that they are minor characters, the Murderers in 3.1 and 3.3 are presented with a great deal of detail. Imagine you were a lawyer defending them in a trial and write up their personal and social backgrounds.

1. Where do they come from, what are their political beliefs, their private fears?
2. What part does Macbeth play in their lives? Is he to blame for their murdering Banquo?

The tide is turning

Sum up Macbeth's situation at the end of act three and contrast it with the end of act two:

1. What has he gained, what has he lost?
2. What is his state of mind?
3. What do his subjects think about him? You will find implicit evidence in 3.4 and explicit and implicit evidence in 3.6.

Act Four

Start here

Know your future

Macbeth is, among other things, a play about people's desire to 'look into the seeds of time' (1.3.56) – an age-old human endeavour.

1. How many different ways and means can you think of, by which people in the past and today have tried to find out about the future?
2. You will probably agree that some of these ways and means are superstitious, some scientific – but how successful are they *really*?
3. Do you think that this issue has a moral aspect, i.e. that there are situations in which people should not try to see into the future?

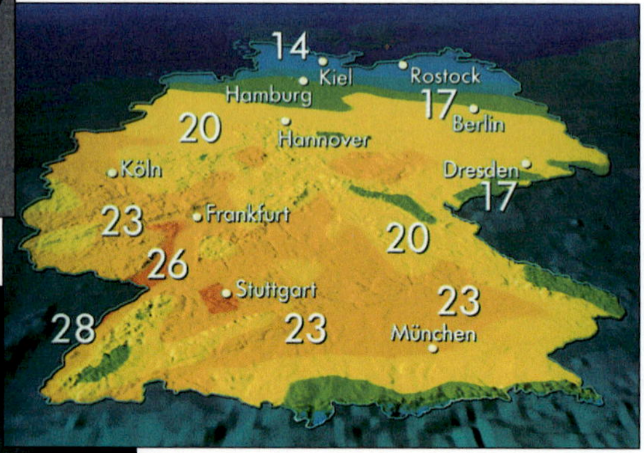

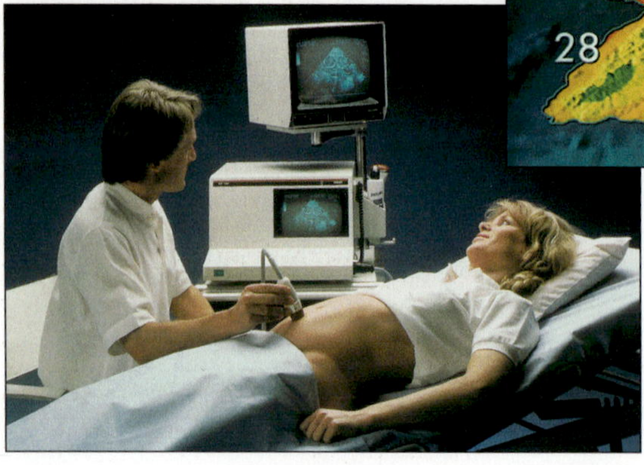

Act 4 Scene 1

In many Elizabethan plays we find supernatural figures, such as devils and demons, ghosts or gods.

1. Do you think it is difficult for a modern audience to accept these figures?
2. How is the supernatural presented in TV or cinema films popular today?

Macbeth joins a meeting of the Weird Sisters. He demands to know what his future will bring. Three apparitions seem to assure him of his invincibility, but another show of spirits reaffirms the fact that Banquo's sons will be kings. Instead of discouraging Macbeth, this encounter reduces his scruples about using violence still further. When he hears that Macduff has fled to England, he decides to have Macduff's family murdered.

The far side

Thunder. Enter the three WITCHES [*with a cauldron*]

FIRST WITCH Thrice* the brindled* cat hath mewed.

SECOND WITCH Thrice and once the hedge-pig* whined.

THIRD WITCH Harpier* cries, ''Tis time. 'tis time.'

FIRST WITCH Round about the cauldron* go;
In the poisoned entrails throw.
Toad, that under cold stone
Days and nights has thirty-one
Sweltered venom* sleeping got,
Boil thou first i'th'charmèd pot.

ALL Double, double toil and trouble;
Fire burn, and cauldron bubble.

SECOND WITCH Fillet of a fenny snake,
In the cauldron boil and bake:
Eye of newt, and toe of frog,
Wool of bat, and tongue of dog,
Adder's fork, and blind-worm's sting,
Lizard's leg, and howlet's wing,
For a charm of powerful trouble,
Like a hell-broth, boil and bubble.

ALL Double, double toil and trouble,
Fire burn, and cauldron bubble.

THIRD WITCH Scale of dragon, tooth of wolf,
Witches' mummy, maw and gulf

Thrice Three times
brindled striped
hedge-pig hedgehog
Harpier spirit in the shape of a harpy (cf. Paddock and Graymalkin in 1.1)
cauldron big pot
Sweltered venom Sweated poison

'Fire burn, and cauldron bubble.' Elizabethan woodcut

Why would an Elizabethan ➢ audience think that Jews, Turks and Tartars are appropriate ingredients for a 'hellish' stew?

gruel soupy mixture
slab thick, sticky

Of the ravined salt-sea shark,
Root of hemlock, digged i'th'dark;
Liver of blaspheming Jew,
Gall of goat, and slips of yew,
Slivered in the moon's eclipse;
Nose of Turk, and Tartar's lips,
Finger of birth-strangled babe,
Ditch-delivered by a drab,
Make the gruel* thick and slab*.
Add thereto a tiger's chawdron
For th'ingredience of our cauldron.

ALL Double, double toil and trouble,
Fire burn, and cauldron bubble.

SECOND WITCH Cool it with a baboon's blood,
Then the charm is firm and good.

Enter HECATE, *and the other three Witches*

pains efforts

HECATE O well done! I commend your pains*,
And every one shall share i'th'gains;
And now about the cauldron sing
Like elves and fairies in a ring,
Enchanting all that you put in.

Music, and a song, 'Black spirits, etc.'
[*Exeunt Hecate and the other three Witches*]

SECOND WITCH By the pricking of my thumbs,
Something wicked this way comes;
Open locks, whoever knocks.

Enter MACBETH

MACBETH How now, you secret, black, and midnight hags!
What is't you do?

ALL THE WITCHES A deed without a name.

to conjure to command (evil) spirits to appear

MACBETH I conjure* you by that which you profess,
Howe'er you come to know it, answer me.
Though you untie the winds and let them fight
Against the churches, though the yeasty waves
Confound and swallow navigation up,
Though bladed corn be lodged and trees blown down,
Though castles topple on their warders' heads,
Though palaces and pyramids do slope
Their heads to their foundations, though the treasure
Of nature's germen* tumble altogether
Even till destruction sicken; answer me
To what I ask you.

nature's germen the seeds of life

FIRST WITCH Speak.

SECOND WITCH Demand.

THIRD WITCH We'll answer.

FIRST WITCH Say, if thou'dst rather hear it from our mouths,
Or from our masters'*?

MACBETH Call 'em, let me see 'em.

FIRST WITCH Pour in sow's blood, that hath eaten
Her nine farrow*; grease that's sweaten
From the murderer's gibbet* throw
Into the flame.

ALL THE WITCHES Come high or low:
Thyself and office* deftly show.

Thunder. [Enter] FIRST APPARITION, *an armed* Head*

MACBETH Tell me, thou unknown power –

FIRST WITCH He knows thy thought;
Hear his speech, but say thou nought.

FIRST APPARITION Macbeth, Macbeth, Macbeth: beware Macduff,
Beware the Thane of Fife. Dismiss me. Enough. *Descends**

MACBETH Whate'er thou art, for thy good caution*, thanks;
Thou hast harped* my fear aright. But one word more –

FIRST WITCH He will not be commanded. Here's another,
More potent* than the first.

Thunder. [Enter] SECOND APPARITION, *a bloody Child*

SECOND APPARITION Macbeth, Macbeth, Macbeth.

MACBETH Had I three ears, I'd hear thee.

SECOND APPARITION Be bloody, bold, and resolute; laugh to scorn
The power of man, for none of woman born
Shall harm Macbeth. *Descends*

MACBETH Then live, Macduff, what need I fear of thee?
But yet I'll make assurance double sure
And take a bond of fate: thou shalt not live,
That I may tell pale-hearted fear it lies,
And sleep in spite of thunder.

Thunder. [Enter] THIRD APPARITION, *a Child crowned, with a tree in his hand*

What is this,
That rises like the issue* of a king
And wears upon his baby-brow the round
And top of sovereignty*?

ALL THE WITCHES Listen, but speak not to't.

THIRD APPARITION Be lion-mettled*, proud, and take no care
Who chafes, who frets*, or where conspirers are.
Macbeth shall never vanquished* be until

our masters' i.e. the demons they serve

≺ Can you guess who the Sisters' 'masters' might be?

farrow piglets
gibbet gallows

office intention, purpose

armed with helmet

Descends i.e. vanishes through a trap door
caution warning
harped guessed

potent powerful

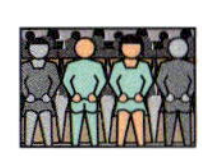

Val: Was that supposed to be a joke? Well, we haven't had many in this play.

issue child

the round ... sovereignty a crown

lion-mettled lion-hearted, brave
chafes ... frets is dissatisfied with your rule
vanquished defeated

'None of woman born shall harm Macbeth.' From a 1976 Royal Shakespeare Company production

Dunsinane Macbeth's castle

to impress to force to march as soldiers
bodements prophecies

lease of nature the natural length of life

I … satisfied I want to hear an answer to my question

Great Birnam Wood to high Dunsinane* hill
Shall come against him. *Descends*

MACBETH That will never be:
Who can impress* the forest, bid the tree
Unfix his earthbound root? Sweet bodements*, good.
Rebellious dead, rise never till the wood
Of Birnam rise, and our high-placed Macbeth
Shall live the lease of nature*, pay his breath
To time and mortal custom. Yet my heart
Throbs to know one thing. Tell me, if your art
Can tell so much, shall Banquo's issue ever
Reign in this kingdom?

ALL THE WITCHES Seek to know no more.

MACBETH I will be satisfied*. Deny me this,
And an eternal curse fall on you. Let me know.
[*Cauldron descends.*] *Hautboys*
Why sinks that cauldron? And what noise is this?

FIRST WITCH Show!

SECOND WITCH Show!

THIRD WITCH Show!

ALL THE WITCHES Show his eyes and grieve* his heart,
Come like shadows, so depart.

*[Enter] a show of eight kings, and [the] last with a glass**
in his hand [Banquo's Ghost following]

MACBETH Thou art too like the spirit of Banquo. Down!
Thy crown does sear* mine eyeballs. And thy hair,
Thou other gold-bound brow, is like the first;
A third, is like the former. – Filthy hags,
Why do you show me this? – A fourth? Start*, eyes!
What, will the line stretch out to th'crack of doom?
Another yet? A seventh? I'll see no more.
And yet the eighth appears, who bears a glass
Which shows me many more. And some I see,
That two-fold balls and treble sceptres* carry.
Horrible sight! Now I see 'tis true,
For the blood-boltered Banquo smiles upon me,
And points at them for his*.
[Exeunt show of kings and Banquo's Ghost]
What, is this so?

FIRST WITCH Ay, sir, all this is so. But why
Stands Macbeth thus amazedly?
Come, sisters, cheer we up his sprites,
And show the best of our delights.
I'll charm the air to give a sound,
While you perform your antic round*
That this great king may kindly say,
Our duties did his welcome pay.
Music. The Witches dance, and vanish

MACBETH Where are they? Gone? Let this pernicious hour,
Stand aye* accursèd in the calendar.
Come in, without there!

Enter LENNOX

LENNOX What's your grace's will?

MACBETH Saw you the weird sisters?

LENNOX No, my lord.

MACBETH Came they not by you?

LENNOX No indeed, my lord.

MACBETH Infected be the air whereon they ride,
And damned all those that trust them. I did hear
The galloping of horse. Who was't came by?

LENNOX 'Tis two or three, my lord, that bring you word
Macduff is fled to England.

MACBETH Fled to England?

LENNOX Ay, my good lord.

to grieve to cause pain to

glass crystal ball

to sear to burn

Start Pop out

two-fold … sceptres two golden balls and three sceptres

his i.e. male descendants (cf. the Scottish royal family tree on p. 21)

⮜ What is Macbeth summing up in this short and simple question?

antic round mad dance in a circle

⮜ What should the music and the dance be like? Slow, fast, crazy, beautiful, noisy …?

aye for ever

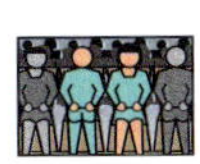

Ian: Wait a minute – the last time we saw Lennox, he practically admitted that he hated Macbeth! What's he doing here now?

Time … exploits Events have prevented me from carrying out my terrible intentions. (Macbeth had just decided to kill Macduff.)
firstlings first-borns
The very … hand I'll carry out all my intentions as soon as I think of them.

sights demonic apparitions

MACBETH [*Aside*] Time, thou anticipat'st my dread exploits*;
The flighty purpose never is o'ertook
Unless the deed go with it. From this moment,
The very firstlings* of my heart shall be
The firstlings of my hand*. And even now
To crown my thoughts with acts, be it thought and done.
The castle of Macduff I will surprise;
Seize upon Fife; give to th'edge o'th'sword
His wife, his babes, and all unfortunate souls
That trace him in his line. No boasting like a fool;
This deed I'll do before this purpose cool,
But no more sights*. – Where are these gentlemen?
Come, bring me where they are.

Exeunt

Royal performance I: A theatrical anecdote describes how, when *Macbeth* was performed before King James I at court, the eighth king carried a mirror which he held in front of James's face. James was the latest in the line of the 'many more' kings descended from Banquo.

Royal performance II: King James I claimed to rule three kingdoms: Great Britain, France and Ireland; the three sceptres may refer to this. The two orbs may signify England and Scotland.

Activities

Demonic cookery

There are many unfamiliar words in the first forty lines of the scene, but you probably got the idea: what the witches are using as ingredients for their stew are the most disgusting or frightening bits of the most disgusting or frightening animals.

1. See which animals or body parts you can identify. Which are disgusting, which frightening?
2. Do you know any stories or myths in folklore in which these animals appear? What is their function and meaning in these stories?

Interpreting the signs

Take a closer look at the supernatural apparitions in this scene:

1. How many are there, and what shapes do they take?
2. At which points in the scene do they appear?
3. What meaning does Macbeth ascribe to them?

To find out the worst

This scene shows the second encounter between Macbeth and the Weird Sisters. One – central – difference is that this time he goes to seek them out, whereas the first time he had no idea of their existence. What other differences, as well as similarities, can you discover between the two scenes? These question may be helpful:

1. What did Macbeth do before he met the Sisters? What is his state of mind?
2. How does he behave towards them? How do they behave towards him?
3. What does he want from them? Does he obtain it?
4. What are the elements of *paradox in both scenes?
5. What are his thoughts and feelings upon leaving the Sisters?
6. What is a theatre audience likely to think and feel about the two scenes in general, and Macbeth's behaviour in particular?

'How now, you secret, black, and midnight hags!' Art nouveau painting and theatre poster, early 20th century

Act 4 Scene 2

Women and children, too

In the following scene Shakespeare shows us an innocent child and his mother as victims of a tyrant. Think of similar situations in history or recent politics.

Lady Macduff complains to Ross about her husband's sudden departure from Scotland, which feels to her like a betrayal. Her conversation with her young son is interrupted by the arrival of the killers Macbeth has sent.

Enter [LADY MACDUFF], *her* SON, *and* ROSS

LADY MACDUFF What had he* done, to make him fly the land?

ROSS You must have patience, madam.
LADY MACDUFF He had none;

he i.e. her husband

wants … touch lacks natural feelings (of a father for his family)

coz cousin
school control

fits … season the current violent times

when we … fear when we believe rumours about the things we fear

Ian: Up and down, up or down … That reminds me of Mr Dixon's beloved *Wheel of Fortune!

Why is Ross in such a hurry ➤ to leave?

Things … upward When things are worst, they will either end or get better.
cousin i.e. Lady Macduff's young son
dead (Lady Macduff is speaking metaphorically.)

net … gin various ways of catching birds
Poor Little

His flight was madness. When our actions do not,
Our fears do make us traitors.

ROSS You know not
Whether it was his wisdom or his fear.

LADY MACDUFF Wisdom? To leave his wife, to leave his babes,
His mansion, and his titles in a place
From whence himself does fly? He loves us not.
He wants the natural touch*, for the poor wren,
The most diminutive of birds, will fight,
Her young ones in her nest, against the owl.
All is the fear, and nothing is the love;
As little is the wisdom, where the flight
So runs against all reason.

ROSS My dearest coz*,
I pray you school* yourself. But for your husband,
He is noble, wise, judicious, and best knows
The fits o'th'season*. I dare not speak much further,
But cruel are the times when we are traitors
And do not know ourselves, when we hold rumour
From what we fear*, yet know not what we fear,
But float upon a wild and violent sea,
Each way and none. I take my leave of you,
Shall not be long but I'll be here again.
Things at the worst will cease, or else climb upward*
To what they were before. My pretty cousin*,
Blessing upon you.

LADY MACDUFF Fathered he is, and yet he's fatherless.

ROSS I am so much a fool, should I stay longer
It would be my disgrace and your discomfort.
I take my leave at once. *Exit*

LADY MACDUFF Sirrah, your father's dead*,
And what will you do now? How will you live?

SON As birds do, mother.

LADY MACDUFF What, with worms and flies?

SON With what I get I mean, and so do they.

LADY MACDUFF Poor bird, thou'dst never fear the net, nor lime,
the pitfall, nor the gin*.

SON Why should I, mother? Poor* birds they are not set for.
My father is not dead for all your saying.

LADY MACDUFF Yes, he is dead. How wilt thou do for a father?

SON Nay, how will you do for a husband?

LADY MACDUFF Why, I can buy me twenty at any market.
SON Then you'll buy 'em to sell again.

LADY MACDUFF Thou speak'st with all thy wit*, and yet i'faith with wit enough for thee.

SON Was my father a traitor, mother?

LADY MACDUFF Ay, that he was*.

SON What is a traitor?

LADY MACDUFF Why, one that swears and lies.

SON And be all traitors, that do so?

LADY MACDUFF Every one that does so is a traitor and must be hanged.

SON And must they all be hanged that swear and lie?

LADY MACDUFF Every one.

SON Who must hang them?

LADY MACDUFF Why, the honest men.

SON Then the liars and swearers are fools, for there are liars and swearers enough to beat the honest men and hang up them.

LADY MACDUFF Now God help thee, poor monkey, but how wilt thou do for a father?

SON If he were dead, you'd weep for him; if you would not, it were a good sign that I should quickly have a new father.

LADY MACDUFF Poor prattler, how thou talk'st!

Enter a MESSENGER

MESSENGER Bless you, fair dame. I am not to you known,
Though in your state of honour I am perfect;
I doubt some danger does approach you nearly.
If you will take a homely man's advice,
Be not found here. Hence with your little ones.
To fright you thus, methinks I am too savage;
To do worse to you were fell cruelty,
Which is too nigh* your person. Heaven preserve you,
I dare abide no longer. *Exit*

LADY MACDUFF Whither should I fly?
I have done no harm. But I remember now
I am in this earthly world where to do harm
Is often laudable*, to do good sometime
Accounted dangerous folly. Why then, alas,
Do I put up that womanly defence,
To say I have done no harm?

Enter MURDERERS

What are these faces?

A MURDERER Where is your husband?

wit intelligence (here, precociousness)

Ay ... was i.e. to his family

➤ What do you think of this piece of cynicism from a child's mouth?

nigh near

laudable praiseworthy

'He has killed me, mother.' From Polanski's film (1971)

unsanctified unholy

shag-haired with long, untidy hair

fry young fish

LADY MACDUFF I hope in no place so unsanctified*,
Where such as thou mayst find him.

A MURDERER He's a traitor.

SON Thou liest, thou shag-haired* villain.

A MURDERER What, you egg!
Young fry* of treachery!
[*Kills him*]

SON He has killed me, mother,
Run away, I pray you!
Exit [*Lady Macduff*] *crying 'Murder'* [*, pursued by Murderers with her Son*]

Activities

A moral problem

Ross is sympathetic to Lady Macduff's plight, yet at the same time he seems to understand Macduff's decision to leave the country. Are there two sides to Macduff's behaviour? He must have known that his flight would put his family into extreme danger, so evidently there was something that was even more important to him than his wife and children.

1. Write a scene that Shakespeare did not consider necessary for this play: a discussion between Lady Macduff and Macduff about whether he should stay at home to protect his family, or join Prince Malcolm at the English court.
2. There are several important scenes in this play in which a married couple is shown quarrelling. What might have been Shakespeare's reason for *not* writing such a scene for the Macduffs?

And another blood-bath

This is the second time in the play that a murder is shown onstage. Compare the murder of Banquo with the murder of the Macduffs for their dramatic structure and effect:

1. Who and what are the killers, who and what are the victims?
2. Why do the victims have to die?
3. Whose perspective do the scenes take? What is the atmosphere?
4. What are the victims talking about when they are surprised?
5. What sort of violence does the text specify or imply?
6. Many readers feel – and theatre productions usually bear this out – that the murder of the Macduffs is the more shocking of the two. Do you agree? Give reasons.

Act 4 Scene 3

Friend or foe?

Imagine yourself in a situation where you desperately need a person you can rely on. How would you find out whether a friend can be trusted?

At the English court, Malcolm and Macduff lament the tyrannous rule Scotland has to suffer; but each man is wary of the other and tries to draw him out. As a test for Macduff's honesty, Malcolm pretends to confess that he would be an even crueller tyrant than Macbeth.
Ross enters with the news of the latest murders. They all swear to join forces and to fight for Macbeth's overthrow.

Enter MALCOLM *and* MACDUFF

MALCOLM Let us seek out some desolate shade* and there
Weep our sad bosoms empty.

MACDUFF Let us rather
Hold fast* the mortal* sword and like good men
Bestride our downfall birthdom*; each new morn,
New widows howl, new orphans cry, new sorrows
Strike heaven on the face, that it resounds
As if it felt with Scotland and yelled out
Like syllable of dolour*.

desolate shade lonely place

fast tightly
mortal fatal
Bestride ... birthdom Stand over our injured country (as a soldier over a fallen comrade)

Like ... dolour Similar cry of pain

MALCOLM What I believe, I'll wail*;
What know, believe; and what I can redress,
As I shall find the time to friend, I will*.
What you have spoke, it may be so perchance*.
This tyrant, whose sole name blisters our tongues,
Was once thought honest; you have loved him well –
He hath not touched you yet. I am young, but something
You may discern of him through me*, and wisdom
To offer up a weak, poor, innocent lamb
T'appease an angry god.

MACDUFF I am not treacherous.

MALCOLM But Macbeth is.
A good and virtuous nature may recoil
In an imperial charge*. But I shall crave your pardon:
That which you are, my thoughts cannot transpose*;
Angels are bright still, though the brightest* fell.
Though all things foul would wear the brows of grace,
Yet grace must still look so*.

MACDUFF I have lost my hopes.

MALCOLM Perchance even there where I did find my doubts.
Why in that rawness* left you wife and child,
Those precious motives, those strong knots of love,
Without leave-taking? I pray you,
Let not my jealousies* be your dishonours,
But mine own safeties; you may be rightly just,
Whatever I shall think.

MACDUFF Bleed, bleed, poor country.
Great tyranny, lay thou thy basis sure*,
For goodness dare not check* thee; wear thou thy wrongs,
The title is affeered*. Fare thee well, lord,
I would not be the villain that thou think'st
For the whole space that's in the tyrant's grasp,
And the rich East to boot*.

MALCOLM Be not offended.
I speak not as in absolute fear of you:
I think our country sinks beneath the yoke*;
It weeps, it bleeds, and each new day a gash
Is added to her wounds. I think withal*
There would be hands uplifted in my right,
And here from gracious England have I offer
Of goodly thousands*. But for all this,
When I shall tread upon the tyrant's head,
Or wear it on my sword, yet my poor country
Shall have more vices than it had before,
More suffer, and more sundry* ways than ever,
By him that shall succeed.

MACDUFF What should he be?

to wail to mourn, pity

what … will what I can put right, I will – provided the circumstances are right

perchance perhaps

something … me you may think you can gain Macbeth's favour by betraying me

A good … charge A king's command may force even a good man to commit crimes.

Ian: Aha! Here is someone who insists that fair is fair, and foul is foul! That makes a change …

to transpose to change

the brightest Lucifer

What is Malcolm implying ➢ with this question?

Though … look so True moral goodness remains good, even if evil disguises itself as goodness (in order to deceive).

rawness vulnerability (i.e. to Macbeth's violence)

jealousies suspicions

lay … sure don't worry

to check to stop

The title is affeered Your kingship is secure

to boot as well

yoke oppression

withal besides

thousands i.e. of soldiers (not money)

sundry various

MALCOLM It is myself I mean – in whom I know
All the particulars of vice so grafted*
That when they shall be opened, black Macbeth
Will seem as pure as snow, and the poor state
Esteem him as a lamb, being compared
With my confineless harms*.

MACDUFF Not in the legions
Of horrid hell can come a devil more damned
In evils to top Macbeth.

MALCOLM I grant him* bloody,
Luxurious*, avaricious*, false, deceitful,
Sudden, malicious, smacking of every sin
That has a name. But there's no bottom, none,
In my voluptuousness*: your wives, your daughters,
Your matrons, and your maids could not fill up
The cistern of my lust, and my desire
All continent impediments* would o'erbear
That did oppose my will. Better Macbeth,
Than such an one to reign.

MACDUFF Boundless intemperance*
In nature is a tyranny; it hath been
Th'untimely emptying of the happy throne
And fall of many kings. But fear not yet

grafted built in, rooted

confineless harms endless cruelties

grant him admit he's

➤ What are the bad qualities with which Malcolm saddles Macbeth?

Luxurious Lecherous, full of sexual lust
avaricious greedy for money
voluptuousness sexual lust
continent impediments attempts to stop me

Boundless intemperance Uncontrolled sexuality

'O Scotland, Scotland!' Pieter Breughel, *The Triumph of Death* (1562)

you may … cold you may sleep with as many women as you want, and yet seem to be virtuous
to hoodwink to make blind, mislead

How does Macduff respond to Malcolm's confession that he is a ruthless womanizer?

As … themselves As will prostitute themselves to powerful men
ill-composed affection unbalanced character
stanchless unstoppable

to forge to make, provoke

Sticks deeper Is worse
summer-seeming lust lust that will pass when a man becomes older
foison rich harvests
portable bearable, tolerable
With … weighed Considering your virtues

What, according to Malcolm, are the qualifying characteristics of a king?

I … crime I have not the smallest part of these virtues, but many bad qualities
concord harmony
confound destroy

truest issue most rightful heir
interdiction accusation
blaspheme his breed disgrace his family

Died i.e. with hard prayer and religious exercise

To take upon you what is yours: you may
Convey your pleasures in a spacious plenty
And yet seem cold*. The time you may so hoodwink*.
We have willing dames enough; there cannot be
That vulture in you to devour so many
As will to greatness dedicate themselves*,
Finding it so inclined.

MALCOLM With this, there grows
In my most ill-composed affection* such
A stanchless* avarice that, were I king,
I should cut off the nobles for their lands,
Desire his jewels, and this other's house,
And my more-having would be as a sauce
To make me hunger more, that I should forge*
Quarrels unjust against the good and loyal,
Destroying them for wealth.

MACDUFF This avarice
Sticks deeper*, grows with more pernicious root
Than summer-seeming lust*, and it hath been
The sword of our slain kings; yet do not fear,
Scotland hath foisons* to fill up your will
Of your mere own. All these are portable*,
With other graces weighed*.

MALCOLM But I have none. The king-becoming graces –
As justice, verity, temp'rance, stableness,
Bounty, perseverance, mercy, lowliness,
Devotion, patience, courage, fortitude –
I have no relish of them, but abound
In the division of each several crime*,
Acting it many ways. Nay, had I power, I should
Pour the sweet milk of concord* into hell,
Uproar the universal peace, confound*
All unity on earth.

MACDUFF O Scotland, Scotland!

MALCOLM If such a one be fit to govern, speak.
I am as I have spoken.

MACDUFF Fit to govern?
No, not to live. O nation miserable!
With an untitled tyrant, bloody-sceptred,
When shalt thou see thy wholesome days again,
Since that the truest issue* of thy throne
By his own interdiction* stands accursed
And does blaspheme his breed*? Thy royal father
Was a most sainted king; the queen that bore thee,
Oft'ner upon her knees than on her feet,
Died* every day she lived. Fare thee well,
These evils thou repeat'st upon thyself

Hath banished me from Scotland. O my breast,
Thy hope ends here.

MALCOLM Macduff, this noble passion,
Child of integrity, hath from my soul
Wiped the black scruples*, reconciled my thoughts
To thy good truth and honour. Devilish Macbeth
By many of these trains* hath sought to win me
Into his power, and modest wisdom plucks me
From over-credulous haste*; but God above
Deal between thee and me, for even now
I put myself to thy direction and
Unspeak mine own detraction*, here abjure*
The taints and blames I laid upon myself,
For strangers to my nature. I am yet
Unknown to woman, never was forsworn*,
Scarcely have coveted* what was mine own,
At no time broke my faith, would not betray
The devil to his fellow, and delight
No less in truth than life. My first false speaking
Was this upon myself*. What I am truly
Is thine and my poor country's to command:
Whither* indeed, before thy here-approach,
Old Siward with ten thousand warlike men
Already at a point was setting forth.
Now we'll together*, and the chance of goodness
Be like our warranted quarrel*. Why are you silent?

MACDUFF Such welcome and unwelcome things at once,
'Tis hard to reconcile.

Enter a DOCTOR

MALCOLM Well, more anon. –
Comes the king forth, I pray you?

DOCTOR Ay, sir: there are a crew of wretched souls
That stay* his cure; their malady convinces
The great assay of art, but at his touch,
Such sanctity* hath heaven given his hand,
They presently amend*. *Exit*

MALCOLM I thank you, doctor.

MACDUFF What's the disease he means?

MALCOLM 'Tis called the Evil*.
A most miraculous work in this good king,
Which often since my here-remain in England
I have seen him do. How he solicits heaven
Himself best knows, but strangely visited* people
All swoll'n and ulcerous, pitiful to the eye,
The mere despair of surgery, he cures,
Hanging a golden stamp* about their necks

scruples suspicions

trains tricks, schemes (Malcolm thought Macduff had been sent to trick him into admitting that he hates Macbeth.)
modest … haste common sense prevents me from being too trusting
Unspeak … detraction Take back the awful things I said about myself
to abjure to take back
forsworn untruthful
coveted wanted

My first … myself These self-accusations are the first lies I have ever told.
Whither Where

together i.e. fight together against Macbeth
the chance … quarrel may our success be as assured as our cause is just

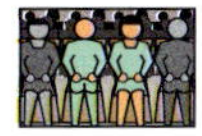

Val: If I were Macduff I would not trust Malcolm anymore. One moment he says he's a devil, the next he's a saint.
Ian: Well, yes, but after all his father was assassinated – he must be careful who he trusts!

to stay to await
sanctity holiness
to amend to get well
Evil i.e. scrofula (Many kings were believed to have the ability to cure this otherwise incurable disease.)

strangely visited incurably ill

stamp coin

Put on with holy prayers, and 'tis spoken
To the succeeding royalty he leaves
The healing benediction. With this strange virtue,
He hath a heavenly gift of prophecy,
And sundry blessings hang about his throne
That speak him full of grace.

Enter Ross

MACDUFF See who comes here.

MALCOLM My countryman, but yet I know him not.

MACDUFF My ever gentle cousin, welcome hither.

Think of possible reasons ➤ why Malcolm did not 'know' Ross at once.

MALCOLM I know him now. Good God betimes remove
The means that makes us strangers.

ROSS Sir, amen.

MACDUFF Stands Scotland where it did?

nothing no one

made, not marked made, but ignored
modern ecstasy general feeling
The deadman's … who When the funeral bell tolls, nobody bothers to ask for whom it tolls.

ROSS Alas, poor country,
Almost afraid to know itself. It cannot
Be called our mother, but our grave, where nothing*
But who knows nothing is once seen to smile;
Where sighs, and groans, and shrieks that rend the air
Are made, not marked*, where violent sorrow seems
A modern ecstasy*. The deadman's knell
Is there scarce asked for who*, and good men's lives
Expire before the flowers in their caps,
Dying or ere they sicken.

relation report
nice detailed, accurate

MACDUFF O relation*
Too nice*, and yet too true.

MALCOLM What's the newest grief?

hiss mock
teems gives birth to

ROSS That of an hour's age doth hiss* the speaker;
Each minute teems* a new one.

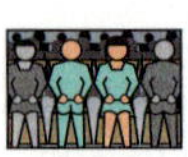

Val: I don't understand how Ross can lie about such a thing!
Ian: He's not lying. He's equivocating …

MACDUFF How does my wife?

ROSS Why, well.

MACDUFF And all my children?

ROSS Well, too.

MACDUFF The tyrant has not battered at their peace?

ROSS No, they were well at peace when I did leave 'em.

MACDUFF Be not a niggard of your speech: how goes't?

tidings news
out i.e. organizing a rebellion
tyrant's power Macbeth's army

ROSS When I came hither to transport the tidings*
Which I have heavily borne, there ran a rumour
Of many worthy fellows that were out*,
Which was to my belief witnessed the rather
For that I saw the tyrant's power* afoot.

Now is the time of help. [*To Malcolm*] Your eye* in Scotland
Would create soldiers, make our women fight
To doff their dire distresses*.

MALCOLM Be't their comfort
We are coming thither. Gracious England* hath
Lent us good Siward and ten thousand men –
An older and a better soldier none
That Christendom gives out.

ROSS Would* I could answer
This comfort with the like. But I have words
That would be howled out in the desert air,
Where hearing should not latch* them.

MACDUFF What concern they?
The general cause, or is it a fee-grief
Due to some single breast*?

ROSS No mind that's honest
But in it shares some woe*, though the main part
Pertains to you alone.

eye person

To doff … distresses To shake off their terrible oppression

Gracious England Good King Edward

Would I wish

latch catch

fee-grief … breast sorrow concerning only one person

woe grief

'All my pretty ones?' Italian Renaissance painting by Guido Reni, *The Slaughter of Children at Bethlehem* (1610)

Genocide's Hall of Shame

From the Ottoman Turkish genocide of 1 million Armenians in 1915 to the 1994 slaughter of 500,000 Rwandan Tutsi – the world had never seen such evil. These men redefined villainy:

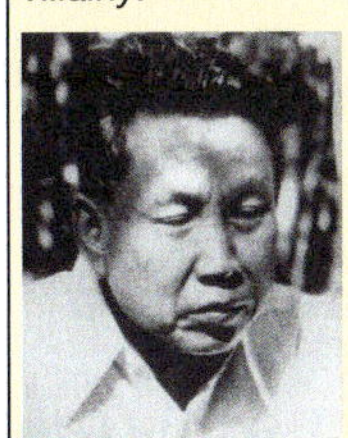

Pol Pot, Cambodia
Number of victims: 2 million. The Khmer Rouge regime killed one quarter of Cambodia's population from 1975 to 1978, targeting almost anyone with a high school education or a pair of glasses

Josef Stalin, Soviet Union
Number of victims: 15 million to 20 million. In the 1930s, Stalin ordered the killing of peasants, collectivization of agriculture and a campaign of famine against Ukraine. By 1933, 11 million people were dead

Idi Amin Dada, Uganda
Number of victims: 300,000. Beginning in 1971, Amin's supporters wrought terror by flagging down cars in broad daylight and locking drivers in the trunks; mutilated bodies would be found the next day floating in rivers

MACDUFF If it be mine,
Keep it not from me; quickly let me have it.

ROSS Let not your ears despise my tongue forever
Which shall possess them with the heaviest sound
That ever yet they heard.

surprised attacked
quarry heap of animals killed in a hunt

MACDUFF H'm – I guess at it.

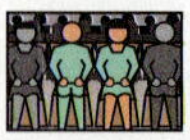
Val: 'Murdered deer'? – How can he play on words in a situation like this? Bad taste, Shakespeare!

ROSS Your castle is surprised*; your wife and babes
Savagely slaughtered. To relate the manner
Were on the quarry* of these murdered deer
To add the death of you.

What, man (Malcolm is addressing Macduff.)
the grief … break if sorrow is not expressed, it will break the heart

MALCOLM Merciful heaven –
What, man*, ne'er pull your hat upon your brows:
Give sorrow words; the grief that does not speak,
Whispers the o'erfraught heart and bids it break*.

MACDUFF My children too?

ROSS Wife, children, servants, all
That could be found.

from thence away from home

MACDUFF And I must be from thence*?
My wife killed too?

ROSS I have said.

MALCOLM Be comforted.
Let's make us med'cines of our great revenge
To cure this deadly grief.

hell-kite bird of prey from hell

'He has no children.' – To whom does 'he' refer, and what does Macduff mean to imply? ➤

fell swoop cruel attack (of a bird of prey, shooting down from above)

MACDUFF He has no children. All my pretty ones?
Did you say all? O hell-kite*! All?
What, all my pretty chickens and their dam
At one fell swoop*?

MALCOLM Dispute* it like a man.

Invent *stage business to fill Macduff's half-line. ➤

to dispute to bear
things people
to take their part to protect them
Naught Sinful
demerits sins

MACDUFF I shall do so;
But I must also feel it as a man;
I cannot but remember such things* were
That were most precious to me. Did heaven look on,
And would not take their part*? Sinful Macduff,
They were all struck for thee. Naught* that I am,
Not for their own demerits* but for mine,
Fell slaughter on their souls. Heaven rest them now.

whetstone sharpener

MALCOLM Be this the whetstone* of your sword, let grief
Convert to anger. Blunt not the heart, enrage it.

braggart show-off
intermission delay
fiend demon

MACDUFF O, I could play the woman with mine eyes
And braggart* with my tongue. But gentle heavens,
Cut short all intermission*. Front to front
Bring thou this fiend* of Scotland and myself;
Within my sword's length set him. If he scape,
Heaven forgive him too.

MALCOLM This tune goes manly.
Come, go we to the king; our power is ready;
Our lack is nothing but our leave. Macbeth
Is ripe for shaking, and the powers above
Put on their instruments. Receive what cheer you may:
The night is long that never finds the day.

Exeunt

Activities

The golden boy?

Actors who have played Malcolm have found it difficult to decide whether he is as honourable and pure-minded as he claims; they have seen him as a rather ambiguous figure.

1. What is your view of Malcolm's 'testing' of Macduff's honesty? Paraphrase his statements in lines 8-24.
   a) What reasons does he give for it?
   b) How does he go about it?
2. How does Macduff react? Has Malcolm manipulated Macduff into compromising himself with his remarks about a king's vices?

Unimaginable horror

Take a closer look at the second half of the scene. Ross enters and has to tell Macduff that his whole family has been butchered.

1. How does he go about relating this dreadful piece of news, and how do the two other men react?
2. What facets of their characters are illustrated by this episode?
3. Once more, the issue of 'manhood' comes up. According to Macduff and Malcolm, how is a man supposed to react when he learns that he has indirectly caused his whole family to be murdered?

Scotland vs. England

Although neither of them is present, this scene implicitly contrasts the English king with the Scottish king.

1. In what ways are the two kings similar, in what ways different?
2. What is each king's relation to supernatural forces?

Reviewing Act Four

Staging the supernatural

Next to the 'banquet scene' (3.4), Macbeth's second meeting with the Weird Sisters (4.1) is the most challenging one to stage in any production of *Macbeth.* Every director has to decide what the three apparitions should look like, and how to present the show of the eight kings. Nor is this only a question of costume: should the 'spirits' be played by actors, or are they puppets, or lighting effects, or something different altogether? In one famous production, Macbeth was given a magic drink and blindfolded: he saw the spirits only in his mind's eye. However you choose to solve this problem, this scene must clarify the nature of the supernatural forces. It is clear that they are strange, otherworldly, and probably demonic – but what do they look like?
Write a director's notes to the set designer, the costume designer, the lighting and sound designer, the actors and the stage manager (the person who makes sure that every prop is ready at the right time and place).

Appearance and identity

The devil was known to Elizabethans as a 'shape-shifter', i.e. one who could change his appearance and metamorphose himself (as the spirits do in 4.1.). Actors, too, were sometimes accused of demonic shape-shifting, especially the younger actors who played women.

1. a) Discuss the sixteenth-century emblem 'Neutrumque et utrumque' ('Neither and both') and the two pictures of *cross-dressers (ill. on p. 93) in the light of two Elizabethan attacks on transvestism and acting:

> 'What man soever weareth womans apparel is accursed, and what woman weareth mans apparel is accursed also. [They] may not improperly be called Hermaphroditi, that is, Monsters of both kindes, half women, half men.'
>
> Philip Stubbes, *Anatomie of Abuses*, 1583, F5v

signes distinctive signs to distinguish

to adulterate to mix up

> 'Garments are set downe for signes distinctive betwene sexe and sexe; to take unto us those garments that are manifest signes of another sexe, is to falsify, forge and adulterate, contrarie to the expresse rule of the words of God.'
>
> Stephen Gosson, *Plays Confuted*, 1582, E1v

A man in woman's dress:
an Elizabethan emblem

Margret Frith, alias Moll Cutpurse, a famous Elizabethan cross-dresser

Make sure that you have exactly described the pictures and understood the quotations before you start comparing them.
b) What is the connection between a person's clothes and his or her identity?

2. Can you imagine what sort of prejudices and anxieties some of Shakespeare's contemporaries had about actors, who dressed up not only as other people but also as persons of the other sex?

3. Discuss the relation between the play's (and the age's) preoccupation with 'disorder', 'reversal of values' and 'confusion' and Elizabethan attacks on transvestism and acting.

François I, King of France (1515-47), in the role of an ancient goddess of war

Act Five

Start here

A debate about rebellion

The first two acts of the play show how Macbeth gains the crown, the last act shows how he loses it again. Regicide, the murder of a king, was almost unanimously denounced by Elizabethans as both the worst kind of crime and the most heinous sin. The question of rebellion, however, was discussed with great heat: Is it permissible for his subjects to overthrow a tyrannous king? Theoretically, rebellion was absolutely forbidden because it disrupts the hierarchy. Practically – and this is certainly the opinion of the rebels in *Macbeth* – it may be the only way to deliver a country from injustice and fear.

What do you think?

Is it morally defensible to steal from a thief?

Can one justify the murder of a king who, in his turn, obtained the crown by murdering a king?

Or are disobedience and the use of force against the order and the head of a state automatically to be condemned?

Again, you may find it helpful to discuss this difficult question by taking examples from history or fiction.

Rebels in space fighting the evil Emperor

W. Churchill, F.D. Roosevelt and J. Stalin in Yalta, 1945

Act 5 Scene 1

Lady Macbeth seems unable to take the strain any more. A doctor and a servant watch her walking and speaking in her sleep. She is racked by feelings of horror and guilt and close to a mental breakdown.

Enter a Doctor *of physic, and a* Waiting-Gentlewoman*

waiting-gentlewoman a female personal servant, often from a noble but impoverished family

Doctor I have two nights watched with you, but can perceive no truth in your report. When was it she last walked?

Gentlewoman Since his majesty went into the field, I have seen her rise from her bed, throw her night-gown upon her, unlock her closet*, take forth paper, fold it, write upon't, read it, afterwards seal it, and again return to bed, yet all this while in a most fast* sleep.

closet small cupboard

fast deep

Doctor A great perturbation* in nature, to receive at once the benefit of sleep and do the effects of watching*. In this slumbery agitation*, besides her walking and other actual performances, what at any time have you heard her say?

perturbation disturbance, abnormality
do … watching act as if one were awake
slumbery agitation sleepwalking

Gentlewoman That, sir, which I will not report after her.

Doctor You may to me, and 'tis most meet* you should.

meet appropriate

Gentlewoman Neither to you, nor anyone, having no witness to confirm my speech.

Enter Lady [Macbeth], *with a taper**

Lo you, here she comes. This is her very guise* and, upon my life, fast asleep. Observe her, stand close*.

taper candle
her very guise her usual behaviour
close hidden

Doctor How came she by that light?

Gentlewoman Why, it stood by her. She has light by her continually, 'tis her command.

➤ Why does she insist on having a candle with her at all times?

Doctor You see her eyes are open.

Gentlewoman Ay, but their sense are shut.

Doctor What is it she does now? Look how she rubs her hands.

Gentlewoman It is an accustomed action with her, to seem thus washing her hands; I have known her continue in this a quarter of an hour.

Lady Macbeth Yet here's a spot.

Doctor Hark, she speaks; I will set down what comes from her to satisfy my remembrance* the more strongly.

satisfy my remembrance support my memory later on

Out Away with you
murky dark
Fie Shame on you
when none … account when no one can demand of us to justify our actions

LADY MACBETH Out* damned spot! Out, I say! One, two. Why then 'tis time to do't. Hell is murky*. Fie*, my lord, fie, a soldier, and afeard? What need we fear? Who knows it, when none can call our power to account*? Yet who would have thought the old man to have had so much blood in him?

DOCTOR Do you mark that?

LADY MACBETH The Thane of Fife had a wife. Where is she now? What, will these hands ne'er be clean? No more o'that, my lord, no more o'that. You mar all with this starting*.

You … starting You ruin everything with your nervous behaviour.
known experienced, done

DOCTOR Go to, go to; you have known* what you should not.

GENTLEWOMAN She has spoke what she should not, I am sure of that. Heaven knows what she has known.

LADY MACBETH Here's the smell of the blood still; all the perfumes of Arabia will not sweeten this little hand. O, O, O.

sorely charged heavy with anxiety

DOCTOR What a sigh is there? The heart is sorely charged*.

I would … body I wouldn't want to suffer like that, even if it meant I could be queen.

GENTLEWOMAN I would not have such a heart in my bosom for the dignity of the whole body*.

DOCTOR Well, well, well –

GENTLEWOMAN Pray God it be, sir.

DOCTOR This disease is beyond my practice; yet I have known those which have walked in their sleep who have died holily in their beds.

'The heart is sorely charged.' Three different ways of playing the sleepwalking scene

LADY MACBETH Wash your hands, put on your night-gown, look not so pale. I tell you yet again, Banquo's buried; he cannot come out on's* grave.

DOCTOR Even so?

LADY MACBETH To bed, to bed; there's knocking at the gate. Come, come, come, come, give me your hand; what's done cannot be undone. To bed, to bed, to bed. *Exit*

DOCTOR Will she go now to bed?

GENTLEWOMAN Directly.

DOCTOR Foul whisp'rings are abroad*; unnatural deeds
Do breed unnatural troubles; infected* minds
To their deaf pillows will discharge their secrets.
More needs she the divine* than the physician*.
God, God forgive us all. Look after her;
Remove from her the means of all annoyance*,
And still keep eyes upon her. So, good night,
My mind she has mated* and amazed my sight.
I think, but dare not speak.

GENTLEWOMAN Good night, good doctor.
Exeunt

out on's out of his

Foul ... abroad Terrible rumours are going round.
infected i.e. with guilt
divine priest
physician doctor
the means ... annoyance all objects with which she might injure herself
mated confused

Paraphrase the doctor's summary of what he has seen and what he thinks of it.

Activities

Sleepwalking

Lady Macbeth's sleepwalking monologue is highly charged with emotion, yet extremely disturbed and fragmented. To explain her jumbled speeches, proceed by several steps:

1. Read out her speech sentence by sentence and decide to whom or what she is referring. Sometimes she addresses her husband and repeats words she has said to him or he to her.
   It will be more lively to do this task as a running commentary by a saner and more truthful *alter ego.* Get together in pairs. One person reads Lady Macbeth's cryptic statements, the *alter ego* supplies a clear explanation or interpretation, e.g. 'Out damned spot' = 'I wish I could wash from my hands the damned blood from the knives with which Macbeth stabbed Duncan, and which I had to carry back into Duncan's room', 'Out, I say!' ='I'm scrubbing as hard as I can, but it won't go away.'
   Compare your 'translation' of her words with the versions of the other groups.
2. What are the thoughts and events that prey most violently on her mind?
3. How do they fit into the themes of the play?

An extract from an autobiography

Thirty years later: the waiting-gentlewoman, now living in comfortable circumstances in a small village in the West of Scotland, is writing her autobiography.
Produce a first-person narrative in which she writes down everything she knew and suspected about the sleepwalking queen, and why she did not say anything at the time.
You are welcome to invent details or background information as long as it doesn't go against the evidence in the play.

Act 5 Scene 2

The rebels are assembling. Other Scottish thanes and the English king have joined them. They sum up their and Macbeth's situation in preparation for the all-decisive battle.

colours banners

their … man their reasons for fighting are so strong that they would make even a dead man join the army

He … rule He cannot control his rebellious kingdom.

Now … faith-breach Every minute more men join the rebellion, as a sign of protest against his regicide.

Drum and colours. Enter* MENTEITH, CAITHNESS, ANGUS, LENNOX, *Soldiers*

MENTEITH The English power is near, led on by Malcolm,
His uncle Siward, and the good Macduff.
Revenges burn in them, for their dear causes
Would to the bleeding and the grim alarm
Excite the mortified man*.

ANGUS Near Birnam Wood
Shall we well meet them; that way are they coming.

CAITHNESS Who knows if Donaldbain be with his brother?

LENNOX For certain, sir, he is not. I have a file
Of all the gentry; there is Siward's son
And many unrough youths that even now
Protest their first of manhood.

MENTEITH What does the tyrant?

CAITHNESS Great Dunsinane he strongly fortifies.
Some say he's mad; others that lesser hate him
Do call it valiant fury, but for certain
He cannot buckle his distempered cause
Within the belt of rule*.

ANGUS Now does he feel
His secret murders sticking on his hands.
Now minutely revolts upbraid his faith-breach*,
Those he commands, move only in command,
Nothing in love. Now does he feel his title

Hang loose about him, like a giant's robe
Upon a dwarfish thief.

MENTEITH Who then shall blame
His pestered senses* to recoil and start,
When all that is within him does condemn
Itself for being there?

CAITHNESS Well, march we on
To give obedience where 'tis truly owed;
Meet we the med'cine of the sickly weal*,
And with him* pour we in our country's purge,
Each drop of us.

LENNOX Or so much as it needs
To dew* the sovereign flower and drown the weeds.
Make we our march towards Birnam.

Exeunt, marching

Val: Have you noticed that the play is full of clothing metaphors?
Ian: Yes, I have, I'm not stupid! Kingship doesn't suit Macbeth – it's too big for him …
Val: The same could be said about your mouth!

pestered senses tortured mind
sickly weal suffering country
him i.e. Malcolm

dew water

Activities

For the third time in the play, we hear a lengthy report about Macbeth's actions from a third party. Read closely the answer to Menteith's question 'What does the tyrant?':

'What does the tyrant?'

1. What is known of Macbeth's actions and his state of mind?
2. How do the thanes interpret these?
3. Compare the Macbeth described in these lines with the Macbeth described in the Messenger's speeches in 1.2. – Is it the same man?

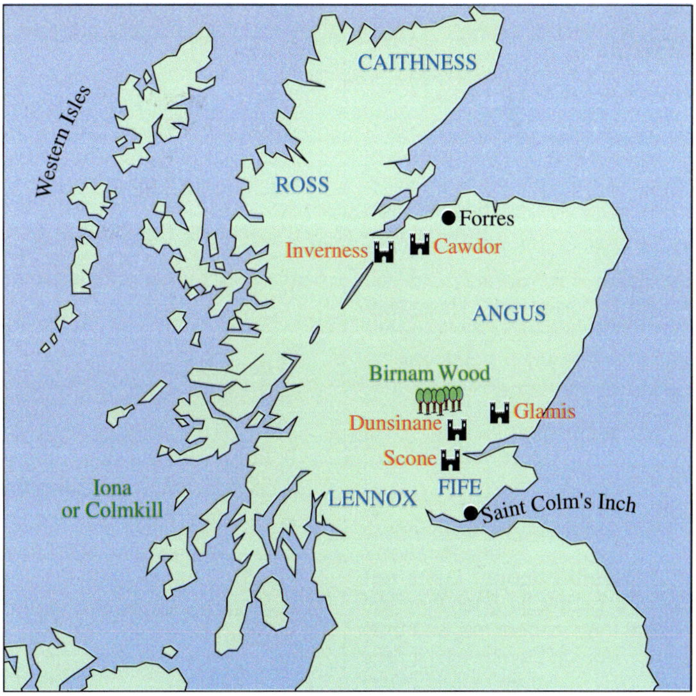

Act 5 Scene 3

Inside the castle. While Macbeth is preparing himself for battle, he receives news of the rebels' progress and of his wife's illness. However, the prophecies of the three apparitions allow him to feel safe.

Enter MACBETH, DOCTOR, *and Attendants*

MACBETH Bring me no more reports, let them fly all;
Till Birnam Wood remove to Dunsinane,
I cannot taint with fear. What's the boy Malcolm?
Was he not born of woman? The spirits that know
All mortal consequences* have pronounced me thus:
'Fear not, Macbeth, no man that's born of woman
Shall e'er have power upon thee.' Then fly false thanes
And mingle with the English epicures*;
The mind I sway* by and the heart I bear
Shall never sag* with doubt nor shake with fear.

mortal consequences the fates of all human beings

epicures 'softies'
sway rule
sag sink

Enter SERVANT

The devil damn thee black, thou cream-faced loon*.
Where got'st thou that goose-look?

loon fool

SERVANT There is ten thousand –

MACBETH Geese, villain?

SERVANT Soldiers, sir.

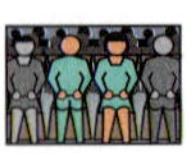

Val: Another joke! Well, sort of … The prospect of death seems to cheer him up …

MACBETH Go prick thy face and over-red thy fear,
Thou lily-livered* boy. What soldiers, patch*?
Death of thy soul, those linen cheeks of thine
Are counsellors to fear. What soldiers, whey-face?

lily-livered cowardly (The liver was believed to be the seat of courage; a bloodless liver is white as a lily.)
patch clown

SERVANT The English force, so please you.

MACBETH Take thy face hence!

[*Exit Servant*]

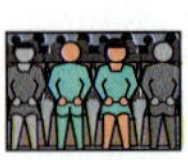

Ian: *'Satan'?* Did you hear that? He called the servant 'Satan'!
Val: Calm down, it's only the sound of the name.

Seyton! – I am sick at heart,
When I behold – Seyton, I say! – this push*
Will cheer me ever or disseat me now.
I have lived long enough. My way of life
Is fall'n into the sere*, the yellow leaf,
And that which should accompany old age,
As honour, love, obedience, troops of friends,
I must not look to have; but in their stead,
Curses, not loud but deep, mouth-honour, breath
Which the poor heart would fain deny, and dare not*.
Seyton!

push effort (i.e. the battle)
sere withered, dry

How does Macbeth assess his situation?

mouth-honour … dare not i.e. people lie when they say that they respect me; and they wouldn't even say it if they weren't afraid of me

Enter SEYTON

SEYTON What's your gracious pleasure?

MACBETH What news more?

SEYTON All is confirmed, my lord, which was reported.

MACBETH I'll fight till from my bones my flesh be hacked.
Give me my armour.

SEYTON 'Tis not needed yet.

MACBETH I'll put it on;
Send out more horses; skirr the country round.
Hang those that talk of fear. Give me mine armour.
How does your patient, doctor?

DOCTOR Not so sick, my lord,
As she is troubled with thick-coming fancies*
That keep her from her rest.

MACBETH Cure her of that.
Canst thou not minister* to a mind diseased,
Pluck from the memory a rooted sorrow,
Raze* out the written troubles of the brain,
And with some sweet oblivious antidote
Cleanse the stuffed bosom* of that perilous stuff
Which weighs upon the heart?

DOCTOR Therein the patient
Must minister to himself.

MACBETH Throw physic* to the dogs, I'll none of it.
Come, put mine armour on; give me my staff. –
Seyton, send out*. – Doctor, the thanes fly from me. –
[*To Attendant*] Come sir, dispatch. – If thou couldst, doctor, cast
The water* of my land, find her disease,
And purge it to a sound and pristine health,
I would applaud thee to the very echo
That should applaud again. – Pull't off, I say*! –
What rhubarb, cynne, or what purgative drug
Would scour* these English hence? Hear'st thou of them?

DOCTOR Ay, my good lord; your royal preparation
Makes us hear something.

MACBETH Bring it* after me. –
I will not be afraid of death and bane*,
Till Birnam Forest come to Dunsinane.
[*Exeunt all but Doctor*]

DOCTOR Were I from Dunsinane away and clear,
Profit again should hardly draw me here. *Exit*

Val: 'Hang those that talk of fear.' – That's what the Nazis did at the end of the war ...

thick-coming fancies many nightmares

to minister to cure

Raze Erase

stuffed bosom heavy heart

physic medicine

send out i.e. give out the signal for my soldiers to arm

cast / The water analyse the urine (common diagnostic method at the time)

Pull't off, I say (Macbeth is making an impatient comment on Seyton's efforts to arm him.)

scour chase away

it i.e. the rest of the armour

bane death

Activities

A study in fear

Macbeth has been called 'a study in fear'. Write an essay about the evidence of fear in this scene:

1. How does Macbeth react to the events around him? What does he have to say about fear? Does his behaviour bear out his words?
2. What reasons do the Servant and Seyton have to be afraid?
3. How do the Scottish people behave at this time of unrest?
4. Do you find that what you see and hear in this scene corresponds with the report the thanes give in the previous scene about Macbeth and the state of his country?

'Hang those that talk of fear.' Jacques Callot, 'Der Galgenbaum' (1633)

Act 5 Scene 4

Outside the castle. Order is given to the soldiers to cut off boughs from the trees and, as camouflage, hide beneath them as they approach the castle.

Drum and colours. Enter MALCOLM, SIWARD, MACDUFF, *Siward's son,* MENTEITH, CAITHNESS, ANGUS, *and* SOLDIERS, *marching*

MALCOLM Cousins, I hope the days are near at hand
That chambers* will be safe.

MENTEITH We doubt it nothing*.

SIWARD What wood is this before us?

MENTEITH The Wood of Birnam.

MALCOLM Let every soldier hew him down a bough*,
And bear't before him; thereby shall we shadow*
The numbers of our host and make discovery
Err in report of us.

chambers bedrooms (Evidently it is common knowledge now that it was Macbeth who murdered Duncan in his bed.)
nothing not

hew … bough cut down a small branch of a tree
shadow conceal

A SOLDIER It shall be done.

SIWARD We learn no other but the confident tyrant
Keeps still in Dunsinane and will endure
Our setting down before't*.

MALCOLM 'Tis his main hope,
For where there is advantage to be given,
Both more and less have given him the revolt*,
And none serve with him but constrainèd things*
Whose hearts are absent too.

MACDUFF Let our just censures
Attend the true event and put we on
Industrious soldiership.

SIWARD The time approaches
That will with due decision make us know
What we shall say we have and what we owe;
Thoughts speculative their unsure hopes relate,
But certain issue strokes must arbitrate*.
Towards which, advance the war.

Exeunt, marching

endure ... before't allow us to set up our army around it (in order to attack)

where ... revolt as soon as they got the chance, both captains and ordinary soldiers deserted
constrainèd things men forced to serve as soldiers

Thoughts ... arbitrate Our guesses at the outcome of the battle only show that we can't know for sure; but we'll know for sure once we start fighting.

Activities

Fate is against Macbeth

There is a clue in this scene that allows the audience to guess that Macbeth's fate is sealed, and that he will die. What is it?

Act 5 Scene 5

Inside the castle. Macbeth is told of the death of his wife, but he's too disillusioned to care. Birnam Wood seems to be moving towards the castle. Macbeth fights his panic by entering the battle.

Enter MACBETH, SEYTON, *and Soldiers, with drum and colours*

MACBETH Hang out our banners on the outward walls;
The cry is still, 'They come.' Our castle's strength
Will laugh a siege* to scorn; here let them lie

siege when an army surrounds a castle and waits for it to surrender

ague fever
forced reinforced

Till famine and the ague* eat them up.
Were they not forced* with those that should be ours,
We might have met them dareful, beard to beard,
And beat them backward home.

A cry within of women

What is that noise?

SEYTON It is the cry of women, my good lord.

fell 'fur', i.e. body hair
dismal treatise frightening story
As As if
I … full I'm filled up
Direness Horrors
to start to frighten

MACBETH I have almost forgot the taste of fears;
The time has been, my senses would have cooled
To hear a night-shriek and my fell* of hair
Would at a dismal treatise* rouse and stir
As* life were in't. I have supped full* with horrors;
Direness* familiar to my slaughterous thoughts
Cannot once start* me. Wherefore was that cry?

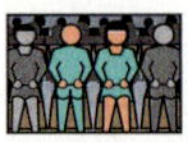

Ian: How does 'Satan' know that? He didn't even leave the stage!
Val: Satan knows everything. Frau Brückenbauer calls it 'satanic omniscience'.
Ian: Well, she should know …

SEYTON The queen, my lord, is dead.

petty pace short, insignificant steps

MACBETH She should have died hereafter;
There would have been a time for such a word.
Tomorrow, and tomorrow, and tomorrow
Creeps in this petty pace* from day to day
To the last syllable of recorded time;
And all our yesterdays have lighted fools
The way to dusty death. Out, out, brief* candle,
Life's but a walking shadow, a poor player*
That struts and frets* his hour upon the stage
And then is heard no more. It is a tale
Told by an idiot, full of sound and fury
Signifying nothing.

brief short
poor player bad actor
struts and frets walks and gesticulates in an exaggerated manner

Enter a MESSENGER

Thou com'st to use thy tongue: thy story quickly.

MESSENGER Gracious my lord,
I should report that which I say I saw,
But know not how to do't.

MACBETH Well, say, sir.

stand my watch stand guard

MESSENGER As I did stand my watch* upon the hill
I looked toward Birnam and anon methought
The wood began to move.

MACBETH Liar and slave!

MESSENGER Let me endure your wrath if't be not so;
Within this three mile may you see it coming.
I say, a moving grove*.

grove wood

MACBETH If thou speak'st false,
Upon the next tree shall thou hang alive
Till famine cling thee; if thy speech be sooth*,
I care not if thou dost for me as much.

sooth truth

I pull in resolution* and begin
To doubt th'equivocation of the fiend
That lies like truth*. Fear not, till Birnam Wood
Do come to Dunsinane', and now a wood
Comes toward Dunsinane. Arm, arm, and out!
If this which he avouches does appear,
There is nor flying hence nor tarrying here*.
I 'gin* to be aweary of the sun
And wish th'estate o'th'world were now undone.
Ring the alarum bell! Blow wind, come wrack*;
At least we'll die with harness* on our back.

Exeunt

I ... resolution I lose confidence

To ... truth To suspect that the devil's ambiguities were lies that sounded like truths

If ... here If the messenger's words are true, there is no point either in fighting or in staying in the castle.
'gin begin
wrack ruin
harness armour

How does Macbeth react to the news that Birnam Wood is coming to Dunsinane?

Activities

The widower

Look at Macbeth's response to the news of his wife's death.

1. First of all, read it out. Pass the speech around: the first person reads only up to the first punctuation mark, then the next person reads up to the second one, etc. Try to read smoothly, but not too fast; give weight to every word, every thought. Take care to emphasize all occurrences of *alliteration.
   What do you think is the tone of this speech? How does it make you feel?
2. What does his first sentence mean? What sort of emotion do his words require from the actor?
3. What are his major metaphors in lines 22-27?
   What is he describing with them?
4. Is it the kind of reaction you would expect from a husband at the news of his wife's death? What is it that makes him react the way he does?

leafy screens camouflage made of leaves

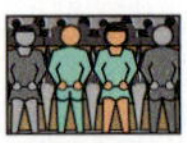

Val: Malcolm lets Siward do all the dirty work!
Ian: Yes, he is a bit of a weasel, isn't he?

Act 5 Scene 6

The rebels ready themselves for combat.

Drum and colours. Enter MALCOLM, SIWARD, MACDUFF, *and their army, with boughs*

MALCOLM Now near enough; your leafy screens* throw down
And show like those you are. You, worthy uncle,
Shall with my cousin your right noble son
Lead our first battle. Worthy Macduff and we
Shall take upon's what else remains to do,
According to our order.

SIWARD Fare you well.
Do we but find the tyrant's power tonight,
Let us be beaten if we cannot fight.

MACDUFF Make all our trumpets speak; give them all breath,
Those clamorous harbingers of blood and death.

Exeunt

Alarums continued

'and now a wood / Comes toward Dunsinane'. From Polanski's film (1971)

Act 5 Scene 7

The battle. Macbeth kills Young Siward. Malcolm swears to be revenged for the deaths of his family.

'I cannot fly.' Scene from a recent film on World War One.

Enter MACBETH

MACBETH They have tied me to a stake; I cannot fly,
But bear-like I must fight the course. What's he
That was not born of woman? Such a one
Am I to fear, or none.

Enter YOUNG SIWARD

YOUNG SIWARD What is thy name?

MACBETH Thou'lt be afraid to hear it.

YOUNG SIWARD No, though thou call'st thyself a hotter name
Than any is in hell.

MACBETH My name's Macbeth.

YOUNG SIWARD The devil himself could not pronounce a title
more hateful to mine ear.

MACBETH No, nor more fearful.

YOUNG SIWARD Thou liest, abhorrèd tyrant; with my sword
I'll prove the lie thou speak'st.

Fight, and Young Siward slain

MACBETH Thou wast born of woman.
But swords I smile at, weapons laugh to scorn,
Brandished by man that's of a woman born.

Exit [*with Young Siward's body*]

Alarums. Enter MACDUFF

MACDUFF That way the noise is. Tyrant, show thy face!
If thou be'st slain*, and with no stroke of mine,
My wife and children's ghosts will haunt me still*.
I cannot strike at wretched kerns* whose arms
Are hired to bear their staves; either thou, Macbeth,
Or else my sword with an unbattered edge
I sheath again undeeded*. There thou shouldst be;
By this great clatter, one of greatest note
Seems bruited. Let me find him, Fortune,
And more I beg not. *Exit*

Alarums. Enter MALCOLM *and* SIWARD

SIWARD This way, my lord; the castle's gently rendered*.
The tyrant's people on both sides do fight;
The noble thanes do bravely in the war.
The day almost itself professes yours,
And little is to do.

MALCOLM We have met with foes
That strike beside us*.

SIWARD Enter, sir, the castle.

Exeunt

Alarum

slain killed
still for ever
kerns foot soldiers
either … undeeded either I fight Macbeth, or I'll put my sword back without having used it

Val: See, Macduff is guilty too, otherwise his family's ghosts wouldn't haunt him!
Ian: I think he's like a ghost himself … – from a revenge tragedy. Searching for the one man he must kill …

gently rendered surrendered without much struggle

That … us Who fight on our side, or: Who deliberately miss us with their swords

Activities

Cornered

Macbeth says he feels like an animal in the popular Elizabethan sport of bear-baiting, in which a bear or a bull were tied up, attacked by dogs and finally torn to pieces. These animal-baiting arenas often doubled as theatres; in fact, situated next to the Globe was a playhouse called the Beargarden.

1. Describe what you can see in the illustration of a bear-baiting arena. What are the similarities between it and a theatre – and between a bear and an actor?
2. What feelings is Macbeth expressing by choosing the bear-baiting metaphor? Turn back to his monologue in 5.5.18-27 to remind yourself of what he had to say about the world as a stage!

'They have tied me to a stake.'
Scene from an animal-baiting arena

Act 5 Scene 8

Showdown between Macbeth and Macduff.

Enter MACBETH

MACBETH Why should I play the Roman fool* and die
On mine own sword? Whiles I see lives, the gashes
Do better upon them.

Enter MACDUFF

MACDUFF Turn, hell-hound, turn.

MACBETH Of all men else I have avoided thee,
But get thee back, my soul is too much charged
With blood of thine* already.

MACDUFF I have no words;
My voice is in my sword, thou bloodier villain
Than terms* can give thee out.

Fight. Alarum

MACBETH Thou losest labour.*
As easy mayst thou the intrenchant air
With thy keen sword impress as make me bleed.
Let fall thy blade on vulnerable crests*;
I bear a charmèd life which must not yield
To one of woman born.

MACDUFF Despair thy charm*,
And let the angel* whom thou still hast served
Tell thee, Macduff was from his mother's womb
Untimely ripped*.

MACBETH Accursed be that tongue that tells me so,
For it hath cowed my better part of man*;
And be these juggling* fiends no more believed
That palter with us in a double sense*,
That keep the word of promise to our ear
And break it to our hope. I'll not fight with thee.

MACDUFF Then yield thee coward*,
And live to be the show and gaze o'th'time*.
We'll have thee, as our rarer monsters are,
Painted upon a pole and underwrit,
'Here may you see the tyrant.'

MACBETH I will not yield
To kiss the ground before young Malcolm's feet
And to be baited with the rabble's* curse.
Though Birnam Wood be come to Dunsinane
And thou opposed being of no woman born,

Roman fool (Roman generals were honour-bound to commit suicide when they lost a battle.)

of thine i.e. of your family

terms words

Thou losest labour You are wasting your time

crests heads

Despair thy charm Forget your magic spells
angel evil angel, i.e. the devil

➤ What effect do Macduff's words have on Macbeth?

Untimely ripped Cut out before time (i.e. Macduff was born by Caesarean section)
cowed … man suppressed my manly spirit

➤ How does Macduff provoke Macbeth into fighting with him?

juggling playing with words
palter … sense trick us with ambiguities
Then … coward Then surrender and admit you're a coward
show … time an exhibition piece for everyone to see
rabble crowd of people

try the last see what I can do by fighting

Yet I will try the last*. Before my body,
I throw my warlike shield. Lay on, Macduff,
And damned be him that first cries, 'Hold, enough!'
Exeunt[,] *fighting. Alarums*

Enter [*Macbeth and Macduff,*] *fighting*[,] *and Macbeth slain*

[*Exit Macduff, with Macbeth's body*]

Activities

Game over

Macbeth finally understands that he has been deceived by the Weird Sisters, whom he now calls 'fiends', i.e. devils. They offered him predictions which he was bound to misinterpret. They did not lie to him, but led him to believe what he wanted to believe; in short, they deceived him with 'equivocations'. Turn back to 4.1 and compare Macbeth's misinterpretations of the apparitions with their true meanings. We can guess now who is the 'child crowned, with a tree in his hand', and who is the 'bloody child'. Only the image of the 'armed head' is still unclear – or is it?

Act 5 Scene 9

The rebels gather after the battle; they have been successful. Macduff enters with Macbeth's head. All rejoice in the death of the tyrant and in the new order they will enjoy under King Malcolm.

Retreat, and flourish. Enter with drum and colours, MALCOLM, SIWARD, ROSS, *Thanes, and Soldiers*

MALCOLM I would the friends we miss were safe arrived.

SIWARD Some must go off*. And yet by these I see,
So great a day as this is cheaply bought*.

Some … off Some are always killed (in war).
cheaply bought won at the cost of few lives

MALCOLM Macduff is missing and your noble son.

ROSS Your son, my lord, has paid a soldier's debt;
He only lived but till he was a man,
The which no sooner had his prowess confirmed

In the unshrinking station where he fought,
But like a man he died.

SIWARD Then he is dead?

ROSS Ay, and brought off the field. Your cause of sorrow
Must not be measured by his worth, for then
It hath no end.

SIWARD Had he his hurts before*?

ROSS Ay, on the front.

SIWARD Why then, God's soldier be he;
Had I as many sons as I have hairs,
I would not wish them to a fairer death.
And so his knell is knolled.

MALCOLM He's worth more sorrow,
And that I'll spend for him.

SIWARD He's worth no more;
They say he parted well and paid his score,
And so God be with him. Here comes newer comfort.

Enter MACDUFF, *with Macbeth's head*

MACDUFF Hail, king, for so thou art. Behold where stands*
Th'usurper's cursèd head. The time is free.
I see thee compassed with thy kingdom's pearl*,
That speak my salutation in their minds;
Whose voices I desire aloud with mine.
Hail, King of Scotland.

before in his chest (Wounds in his back would have meant he was running away.)

stands (Macduff probably has the head stuck on his sword.)
≺ Elaborate on Macduff's laconic statement that 'The time is free'.
compassed ... pearl surrounded by your finest warriors

'Th'usurper's cursèd head.'

ALL Hail, King of Scotland.

Flourish

MALCOLM We shall not spend a large expense of time
Before we reckon with your several loves
And make us even with you. My thanes and kinsmen,
Henceforth be earls, the first that ever Scotland
In such an honour named. What's more to do
Which would be planted newly with the time*, –
As calling home our exiled friends abroad
That fled the snares of watchful tyranny,
Producing forth the cruel ministers*
Of this dead butcher and his fiend-like queen,
Who, as 'tis thought, by self and violent hands
Took off her life, – this and what needful else
That calls upon us, by the grace of Grace
We will perform in measure, time, and place*.
So, thanks to all at once and to each one,
Whom we invite to see us crowned at Scone.

Flourish

Exeunt

What's … time The other things we have to do, now that a new reign has begun

ministers helpers

measure … place in the appropriate order, at the right time and place

Activities

The new king speaks

You have probably heard politicians speak on TV after they have won a general election. They sum up why their party is the best and why the other parties are wrong; then the party leader proceeds to read a declaration of government.

1. Are there elements of propaganda in the last speech of the play? Malcolm's words may well be read in history books of later ages – are his view and interpretation of the events the same as yours?
2. What part does Macduff's speech (21–26) play in Malcolm's accession to power? Remember their encounter in England (4.3)! Remember also the fact that in medieval Scotland it was not the custom that a king was succeeded by his eldest son, but that a new king was elected by the thanes.

Reviewing Act Five

A bleeding country

Imagine you are a foreign war-correspondent who is writing an article for a political magazine in your home country about the insurrection in Scotland. You have been travelling in Scotland for a month, speaking to the people and the rebels. You have also visited the Scottish court and spoken to Scottish refugees living at the English court.

In your article, describe to your readers as clearly and vividly as possible what life in Scotland is like. (You will need evidence from acts four and five.)

1. What is your information about, and impression of, the Scottish king and queen?
2. What are the King's methods of government?
3. What can you tell about public life in Scotland?
4. Report the refugees' experiences as you have been told them. What is your impression of the Scots in England?
5. What is the state of the insurrection?

The themes and images

After act one, you were asked to identify themes and images that might become central to the play's meaning.

1. Which, in your opinion, are the most significant, most interesting, most effective themes and images of act five?
2. Compare your impressions and expectations after act one with your views after having read act five.

Meanwhile ...

When Lady Macbeth enters the stage for her final appearance in the play, the audience has not seen her for quite some time.

1. When did she last appear on stage?
2. What were the circumstances and the context of that appearance?
3. What are her state of mind and the state of her nerves?
4. Compare her presentation in that scene with her presentation in act five. In what ways has she changed?
5. Would you have expected Lady Macbeth to end this way? What do you think of Shakespeare's treatment of her in the second half of the play?

Reviewing the Play

Exit the hero

'At the conclusion of this tragedy, we accept without demur the judgment that Macbeth is a butcher. In fact, however, he is no more a butcher at the end than he is at the beginning. Macbeth lives in a culture that values butchery. Throughout the play manhood is equated with the ability to kill. Power is the highest value in Scotland, and in Scottish culture, power is military prowess.'

(Marilyn French, *Shakespeare's Division of Experience*, Jonathan Cape, London, 1982, p. 243)

1. Find evidence in the play to support this assessment of Macbeth and of Scotland. What does it mean to be a man in Scottish society? There are several passages in the play in which this is explicitly discussed, and you can probably find more passages, in which male identity is an unspoken issue.
2. Which of these criteria of manhood does Macbeth fulfil, with which does he struggle, which does he fail to fulfil?
3. More generally speaking, what are the greatest strengths and weaknesses of his character?
4. It is a proposition accepted by many actors and theatre-goers that the most interesting and appealing qualities of Macbeth are exactly those that stand in contrast to the 'Scottish' concept of manhood. Do you agree with this view? Collect evidence from the play that shows the sensitive, human sides of a man well capable of love, compassion and fear.

Exit the heroine

Dame Ellen Terry (who played Lady Macbeth in 1888, see ill. on p. 7):

'It seems strange to me that anyone can think of Lady Macbeth as a sort of monster, abnormally hard, abnormally cruel, or visualize her as a woman of powerful physique with the muscles of a prize fighter. [...] I conceive Lady Macbeth as a small, slight woman of acute nervous sensibility.'

(Judith Cook, *Women in Shakespeare*, Harrap, London, 1980, p. 127)

1. Find clues in the play to defend either of these two views of Lady Macbeth.

2. How do you see her? Organize a formal debate: one half of the class draws a negative, unattractive image of Lady Macbeth, the other half opposes them by emphasizing her positive, attractive features.
3. In a tragedy that bears her husband's name, Lady Macbeth is the second most important, second most interesting character. What are her functions in the play?
4. Why could the play as it stands not have been called *The Tragedy of Macbeth and Lady Macbeth*?

He has no children

'Lacking children, the Macbeths' energies redirected themselves into obsessions that travestied creativity: they killed other people's children, turning their kingdom into a wasteland. But when they discovered what it meant to hold a barren sceptre, their childlessness doubly mocked them. There could be no success without succession.'

(Carol Rutter et al, *Clamorous Voices. Shakespeare's Women Today*, London 1988, p. 56)

1. Who are the children in this play? List all characters who are *explicitly and significantly* presented as part of a child-parent relationship.
2. Find central or prominent passages in which children are shown, mentioned or discussed, either as actual characters, as an idea, or as a metaphor for something else. What ideas or feelings do the characters in *Macbeth* connect with children?
3. How important is the Macbeths' childlessness for the plot of the play? What do we know about their feelings and opinions about children and the fact that they have none?

Get some therapy!

Imagine you were a family therapist consulted regularly by Macbeth and his Lady from the moment Macbeth had his first vision of witches (or was it a real encounter?). Report to the chairperson of your institution how you tried to help the couple and why it all went wrong.

Things that are seen in the dark

'Now o'er the one half-world / Nature seems dead, and wicked dreams abuse / The curtained sleep.' (2.1.49-51)

Literal and metaphoric darkness descends not only over Scotland, but also over the play *Macbeth.* At least six of its central scenes are set in the dark, many more take place at night. Added to that is a strong preoccupation with sleep, visions and nightmares. Both the Macbeths are unable to sleep peacefully after the murder of the king; their disturbed and guilty minds torture them with visions of the dreadful deeds they have committed.

1. Organize yourselves into five groups, one for each act, and discuss the significance of night, sleep, visions and nightmares in them.
2. Compare your findings with the other groups' and try to come to a final conclusion about the way Shakespeare presents and uses night, sleep, visions and nightmares in the whole play.

A memorial service

Suppose you were a priest asked to prepare a church service in memory of all who died in *Macbeth*. Give an outline of your sermon. Would you include the Macbeths in your prayers? Give reasons.

Casting the actors

Cast the play with actors you know from stage or screen.

1. What are your criteria?
2. Do you choose the actors for their looks or for the characters you have seen them act?

Remember that they must be capable of presenting as many aspects of a character as possible – not just one. Don't forget that actors must not only play their own parts well but also be able to portray their character's relationships with the other characters.

Witchcraft in *Macbeth:* The Weird Sisters

Eleventh-century Scotland and England as Shakespeare portrays them in *Macbeth* are Christian countries, just as they were in his lifetime. But most of Shakespeare's contemporaries, like the characters in *Macbeth*, saw no difficulties in combining a belief in the Christian God with a far older belief in supernatural beings like demons, ghosts and fairies. They took it for granted that all sorts of invisible powers – the play mostly uses the term 'spirits' – watched over human life. It was thought to be possible, with the aid of spells and charms, to conjure* these spirits and to control nature with their help. Some spirits took shape as a cat or toad and acted as 'familiars'* to magicians and 'wise women'. These 'wise women', usually old and without family, were very important in their communities (remember most people lived in small villages): they healed the sick, predicted the future and had good luck charms for all occasions. Their position could be dangerous when they were so poor that they had to beg in order to survive, or when something in the village went wrong, for instance when the harvest failed or when a person or animal died in mysterious circumstances. In these cases, the ensuing conflicts were sometimes 'solved' by accusing the 'wise woman' of having used magic to do damage. (The Latin term for this sort of magic is *maleficium*.) In some cases, the woman was then sentenced to death for being a witch, but usually she was punished in a milder way.

The tens of thousands of women who were burnt as witches in early modern Europe from c. 1450 until the middle of the 18th century (not, as is often believed, in the Middle Ages!) were not primarily accused of malefic acts, i.e. of damaging plant, animal or human by means of magic. They were killed because they were said to have entered a pact with the devil, by which the devil lent them the power to do evil in return for their souls. This belief in devil-worship was fairly new in early modern times, not nearly as old as the belief in nature-magic. It involved large numbers of women who flew through the air or travelled across the water to meet in deserted places by night to worship and have sex with the devil, conspire to overthrow Christendom and commit terrible crimes, like killing babies and cooking them. If you wonder why so many innocent women confessed to these dreadful (and often impossible!) deeds, remember that they were tortured until they did so.

to conjure to command spirits to appear

familiars servant spirits

It was believed that witches were possessed by demons, or could conjure demons to possess others. Two well-known **symptoms of possession** were hallucinatory visions and the inability to pray – does that sound familiar to readers or audiences of *Macbeth?*

Hans Baldung Grien,
'Hexensabbath', 1510

All over Europe, people believed in magic, but not every country adopted the idea of conspiratorial devil-worship and the witches' sabbath. What you have to take into account when looking at the 'weird sisters' in *Macbeth* is the fact that although in Scotland the belief in devil-worship was widespread, in England it was never very popular. The most prominent Scotsman to believe in devil-worshipping witches was King James. In 1597, he wrote a book on witches and devil-worship, called *Daemonologie*. When he became James I of England in 1603, he had the book reprinted in London and tried to enforce severe laws against witches in England, but he met with considerable resistance. Although the English were familiar with the idea of devil-worship, most of them refused to become fanatical or hysterical.

1. Shakespeare works elements of two sorts of witchcraft into his play.
   a) List the characteristics of *maleficium* and of devil-worship as explained above.
   b) Identify them in the play and decide whether Shakespeare stresses one kind more than the other.
2. Connect the play's theme of order vs. disorder with early modern fears of witchcraft and demonism.
3. What part do the Weird Sisters play in the unfolding of Macbeth's fate? Do they ever *lie* to him? Are they, in fact, responsible for his downfall?

Shakespeare's Language

At the beginning of the sixteenth century, educated Englishmen (and the few Englishwomen who were taught to read and write) frowned upon their native tongue as the language of peasants; everyone who had something to say, said it in Latin. Over the next hundred years this disdain changed into the most fervent

enthusiasm; and by the time William Shakespeare was a playwright in London (c. 1588-1614), the English language had become capable of a variety and brilliance that has been unrivalled ever since. The only rule for verbal invention was 'Anything goes': Spelling and grammar were as yet unfixed; and the vocabulary was greatly increased, mainly by words that were newly coined and by loanwords from Latin or French. This verbal inventiveness and flexibility means, however, that Elizabethan heightened* language is often not easy to understand.
Don't be disheartened when you read a passage and you think you don't understand it! Shakespeare's audience consisted of people from all walks of life, all levels of education, and he was popular with them all. He will take you with him and draw you into the story – if you are prepared to listen to him.
With the help of a few basic facts about Elizabethan English and Shakespeare's language, it is often possible to guess at the sense of a passage:

heightened elevated, or more intense than the everyday (It is a more neutral term than 'poetic'.)

1. The syntax of questions ('Know you not he has?', 1.7.30; 'Mean you his majesty?', 2.3.64) and negations ('I think not of them', 2.1.21; 'Fail not our feast', 3.1.29) has more in common with German than with modern English. Literal translation into German is helpful in other cases, too: 'the newest state' (1.2.2-3); 'fought 'gainst my captivity' (1.2.5); 'French hose' (2.3.12).

2. Many words still have their literal meanings which have now become secondary: care-ful = depressed; bloody = of/with blood; sensible = perceived by the senses; success = that which follows (as well as something well done).

3. Shakespeare often says something twice: once with words from the Anglo-Saxon, once with Latin or French loanwords. It is enough to understand either: 'With furbished arms and new supplies of men' (1.2.32), 'bosom franchised and allegiance clear' (2.1.28), 'my hand will rather / The multitudinous seas incarnadine, / Making the green one red' (2.2.65-6).

4. The old verbal endings need not bother you: 'he doth', 'she hath', 'it seemeth' mean the same as 'he does', 'she has', 'it seems'. Sometimes – and the same goes for the èd-endings of participles – Shakespeare uses long endings for emphasis ('abhorrèd tyrant', 5.7.11; 'charmèd life', 5.8.12), sometimes he simply needs another syllable to make up a verse line ('As seemeth by his plight, of the revolt', 1.2.2).

5. 'Thou', 'thy', 'thee', 'thine' are used to social inferiors ('Thou art the best o'th'cut-throats', 3.4.17; 'How wilt thou do for a father?', 4.2.38), as insults ('thou bloodier villain / Than terms can give thee out', 5.8.7-8), and in moments

The English language often has an **Anglo-Saxon** and a **Latin/French** word for (almost) the same thing:
playhouse – theatre
writer – poet
playgoers – audience
manhood – masculinity
pig – pork
bright – intelligent

Other fundamental **structural principles** of Shakespeare's language are **antithesis* and **pun*. Look them up in the glossary!

of personal intimacy ('Thou know'st that Banquo and his Fleance lives', 3.2.37; 'my soul is too much charged / With blood of thine already', 5.8.5-6).

6. Nouns in the plural form can be combined with verb forms in the singular: 'Their drenchèd natures lies as in a death' (1.7.68).

Verse and Prose

Are there any musicians in your class who might verify that the beat of **classical music** is 'dum de dum de', while the beat of **rock music** is 'de dum de dum' …?

Like most of his fellow playwrights, Shakespeare wrote his plays largely in *blank verse. Its regular rhythm of 'dĕ dūm dĕ dūm dĕ dūm dĕ dūm dĕ dūm' resembles not only the human heart beat but also the rhythm of rock'n'roll; and just like rock 'n'roll it was popular because it felt natural. In fact, people often speak blank verse without noticing it: 'My̆ brōthĕr tōld mĕ hē'd bĕ hōme bў fīve', 'Thĕ flīppĭng* cār hăs brōkĕn dōwn ăgāin!', 'Sŏ fāir ănd fōul ă dāy Ĭ hāve nŏt sēen' (1.3.36). You can play around with the rhythm by shifting the stress to another syllable: 'Wātch ōut, hĕ'll gīve yŏu ă tōugh tīme tŏdāy!', 'Ănd māke mў sēatĕd hēart knŏck ăt mў rībs' (1.3.135). In these cases, stressed words are put into positions in the verse line that are normally unstressed, in order to draw particular attention to them.

flipping a slightly more polite version of 'f***ing'
Explain why this line is ➢ almost *onomatopoetic.

Sometimes syllables have to be left out, or 'elided', for the verse line to scan*; this, too, is something we do in everyday speech: 'Mў brōthĕr tōld mĕ hē'd [= he would] bĕ hōme bў fīve', 'Ănd 'tīs [= it is] nŏt dōne; th'ăttēmpt [= the attempt] ănd nōt thĕ dēed' (2.2.10).

scan to be metrically correct; to read metrically

The portion of prose passages differs considerably from one play to the next. In *Macbeth* a mere 145 lines out of 2349 are in prose. The situations and speakers, however, are representative: socially inferior characters usually speak in prose, as do comic characters. Letters are written in prose; and people who are going mad lose not only their minds but also their capacity for the ordered, measured language of verse. On the other hand, when a character who has so far spoken prose suddenly switches to verse, it is a sign to the audience that he or she is making statements of some weight and importance.

1. Pick a passage whose language has seemed very difficult or even incomprehensible. Are the above notes any help in deciphering its meaning?
2. Choose your favourite passage (it should not be shorter than ten lines) and scan it. Which are the words that go against the metrical rhythm?
3. Re-read Macbeth's scene with the murderers (3.1) and the sleepwalking scene (5.1), and explain their changes from prose to verse and from verse to prose.

Macbeth in the Elizabethan Theatre

Shakespeare in the theatre – does that make you think of language that is supposed to be 'poetic' but to you only sounds complicated and old-fashioned? A stage, lit by spotlights, that looks like a living-room with one wall missing? A dark auditorium* that makes you sleepy, uncomfortable seats that keep you awake, people in the next row who hiss at you if you unwrap your chocolate too noisily?

auditorium the main room of a theatre, with stage and seating for the audience

Shakespeare in the theatre – does that make you think, quite frankly, you would rather go to a rock concert or a football match, where you can move about, cheer and hoot at the players, eat, drink, see the other spectators, talk to them and, perhaps, even date them? There was a time when the theatre was a place where you could do all these things. The time is Renaissance England and the places are Elizabethan theatres.

In 1576 a man called James Burbage erected the first purpose-built* theatre, outside London's northern city gates. It had to be outside the city's jurisdiction, because the city authorities did not want the disreputable* playhouses within their walls. Shakespeare came to London some time in the mid- or late 1580s and soon became a shareholder* in Burbage's company, the Lord Chamberlain's Men. Players were energetic, enterprising men: in 1599, when the lease for their theatre ran out, they simply took it to pieces, carted the timber across the River Thames*, and rebuilt it on the southern riverbank. They called their theatre the Globe because, as one of Shakespeare's characters says: 'All the world's a stage, and all the men and women merely players' (*As You Like It*, 2.7.139-40). *Theatrum mundi*:

purpose-built specifically built for one purpose
disreputable of bad reputation

shareholder sb. who owns a share (a portion) of a company or business

Thames [temz]

The Beargarden and the Globe on a Jacobean map of London

the world is a theatre, and the theatre is an image of the world. This idea is mirrored in the terms for stage architecture: the cellar underneath the stage was called 'hell' (one could 'go to hell' by way of a trapdoor), the roof was the 'heavens', and in between the two, human history took its course (cf. ill. on p. 123).

Macbeth was probably written in 1606, but it could not be presented at the Globe straightaway. London was suffering from yet another plague epidemic, and since large crowds of people increased the danger of infection, all theatres had been closed. Legend has it that *Macbeth* was first performed at Hampton Court for King James I, whose servants Shakespeare's company had become in 1603. They were now called the King's Men, which marked them out as the first theatrical company of their time.

One penny was one twelfth of the shilling a skilled craftsman could expect to earn in a day. So the cheapest theatre ticket in 1607 was, relatively speaking, slightly more expensive than a cinema ticket today.

A trip to the theatre in the spring of 1607, when *Macbeth* is likely to have been acted at the Globe, was very different from a trip to the theatre today. To start with, since the stage, the actors (and the audience, too) had to be lit by daylight, performances were given in the afternoon. Large playhouses like the Globe held over 2,000 spectators, and everyone came – but, as in real life, not everyone was equal: ticket prices varied considerably; and the one penny to stand in front of the stage was all a poor apprentice could afford. Yet, even though they did not actually rub shoulders, the audience at an Elizabethan playhouse was a fairly representative cross-section of society. Rich or poor, master or servant, man or woman – every spectator watched not only the players, but also the other spectators' reactions to whatever the players were presenting. An Elizabethan audience was a noisy, rowdy crowd. In order to catch their attention at the beginning of a play, a playwright had to think of an exciting first scene, or the spectators would simply go on chatting to each other.

Do you think the first scene of *Macbeth* is likely to catch the audience's attention? ➤

There was very little scenery* and few props*. The players had swords and armour, torches and candles, severed heads and animal blood, and very colourful costumes. But first and foremost the illusion of a fictional reality was created by the words of the playwright and the imagination of the audience. 'And let us, […] / On your imaginary forces work,' the Chorus in *Henry V* says to the audience and adds: 'Think, when we talk of horses, that you see them' (1.1.17-8, 26). The text of the play tells you everything you need to know in order to visualize the scene – but you must allow it to work on your 'imaginary forces'!

scenery sheets or thin walls at the back of the stage, usually painted and moveable
props movable objects used on stage

Later ages often attempted to recapture the atmosphere and playing conditions of Elizabethan amphitheatres* like the Globe. The most ambitious project so far is the New Globe in London (see ills. on pp. 4 and 5): it stands almost on the exact site of Shakespeare's Globe and aims to be a faithful reconstruction of its great predecessor. Infinite trouble has been taken to ensure authenticity: the building material and build-

amphitheatres round, unroofed theatres

ing techniques, the costumes and acting styles – everything has been carefully researched in order to be as 'Elizabethan' as possible. In 1997 the theatre was finished and has since then presented plays by Shakespeare and his fellow playwrights, in Elizabethan as well as in modern dress.

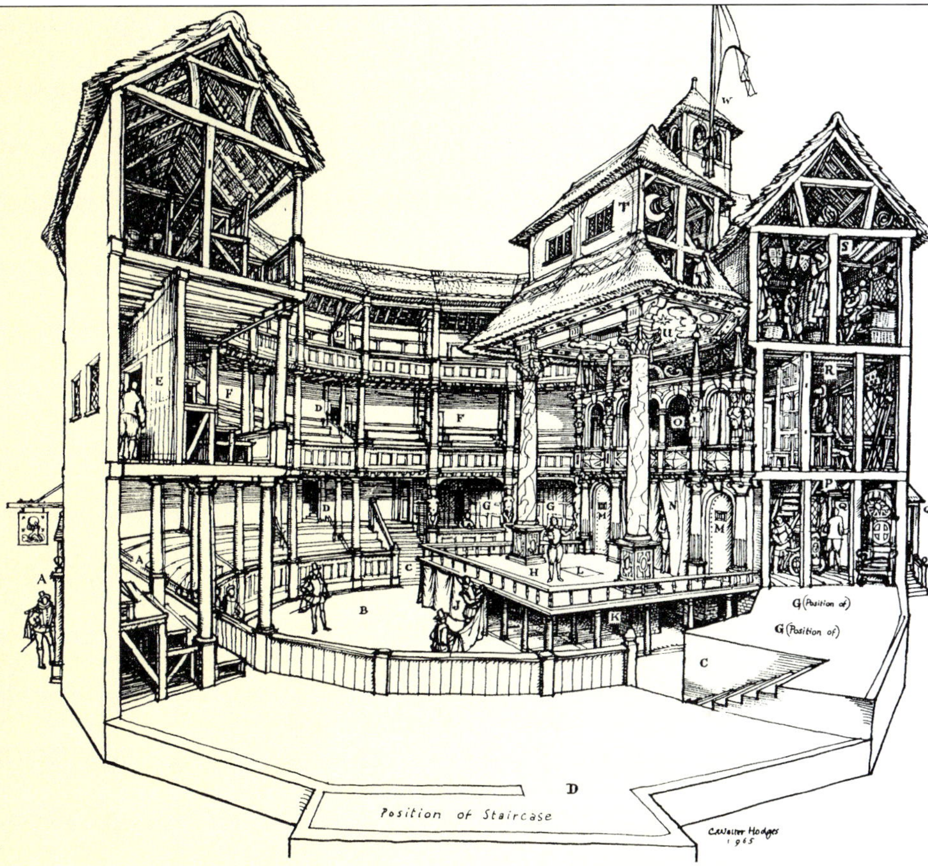

The Globe Playhouse, 1599-1613. A conjectural reconstruction

Key

- AA Main entrance
- B The Yard
- CC Entrances to lowest gallery
- D Entrances to staircase and upper galleries
- E Corridor serving the different sections of the middle gallery
- F Middle gallery ('Twopenny Rooms')
- G 'Gentlemen's Rooms or 'Lords' Rooms'
- H The stage
- J The hanging being put up round the stage
- K The 'Hell' under the stage
- L The stage trap, leading down to the Hell
- MM Stage doors
- N Curtained 'place behind the stage'
- O Gallery above the stage, used as required sometimes by musicians, sometimes by spectators, and often as part of the play
- P Back-stage area (the tiring-house)
- Q Tiring-house door
- R Dressing-rooms
- S Wardrobe and storage
- T The hut housing the machine for lowering enthroned gods, etc., to the stage
- U The 'Heavens'
- W Hoisting the playhouse flag

1. Summarize the conditions and the organization of theatre in London around the time *Macbeth* was first performed.

2. The illustration on p. 123 is a theatre historian's guess at what Shakespeare's Globe may have looked like.
   a) Make yourself familiar with the building with the help of the annotations.
   b) Choose one act of *Macbeth* and speculate on the organization and preparation that must have gone on *behind* the stage while the actors were performing.

3. The New Globe in London has been criticized as a 'museum piece' offering 'Mickey-Mouse Shakespeare'. What do you think of the idea to reconstruct a theatre that burnt down almost 400 years ago, only to present the plays of a playwright who has been dead for almost 400 years?

Tragedy

Like many other important matters, the literary genre called tragedy has undergone various changes and developed a considerable variety of forms during the course of history. The first authors of tragedy in Europe were ancient Greeks: Aeschylos (['i:skɪləs], 525-456 BC), Sophocles (['sɒfəˌkliːz], 469-406 BC) and Euripides ([juˈrɪpɪdiːz], 480-406 BC). Based on the knowledge of their plays, the influential philosopher and literary critic, Aristotle (['ærɪstɒtl], 384-322 BC), described a number of their essentials: apart from the *plot, the **tragic hero/protagonist** was in the centre of Aristotle's interest. He had to be of high rank, usually a king; his character was neither totally bad nor extremely good. Tragedy showed his way from happiness to misery, often his death, caused by some tragic **flaw** or serious error **(hamartia).** Usually this was excessive pride **(hybris),** which led him to ignore warnings. The *tone/atmosphere of tragedy was dignified, its main themes were conflicts, *dilemmas, human suffering. Its intention was to arouse pity and fear and thereby to purify* the spectator from such emotions. The Greek word for purification is **catharsis.**

purify to make clean and wholesome

It was a long way from these early tragedies – and Aristotle's first theory on the genre – to Arthur Miller's relatively recent *Death of a Salesman* (1949), whose 'hero', Willy Loman – pronounced nearly like 'low man' – is far from being a character of high rank, let alone a king.

Somewhere in between these different concepts of tragedy was the medieval notion of the fall of illustrious persons, illustrated in the *wheel of fortune. Medieval tragedies were told rather than performed, as can be deduced from this famous definition taken from Geoffrey Chaucer's (1340-1400) *Canterbury Tales,* written in Middle English (not Old English!):

'Tragedie is to seyn a certyn storie,
As olde bookes maken us memorie,
Of hym that stood in greet prosperitee,
And is y-fallen out of heigh degree
Into myserie, and endeth wreccedly.'

('Tragedy means a certain story as recorded for us in old books about someone who stood in great prosperity and has fallen from his high rank into misery and ends miserably.')

The Middle Ages also tended to mix seriousness with *comic relief, thus giving up the dignified tone of ancient tragedy.

Another important tradition that had a strong influence on Shakespeare's tragedies was the **revenge tragedy**, introduced by the Latin philosopher, tutor of the Emperor Nero (!), and playwright, Seneca (4 BC - 64 AD). An intensified form of the revenge tragedy was the **tragedy of blood** with scenes of assassination and other horrors performed on the stage to satisfy the Elizabethan spectators' appetite for morbid excitement (cf. bear-baiting, public executions etc.).

Shakespeare (1564-1616) produced 37 plays altogether, traditionally divided into three categories of more or less equal size: comedies (the largest group), histories, and tragedies. The latter ones contain elements of the various kinds of tragedy outlined above. Shakespeare's best known tragedies are *Romeo and Juliet, Julius Caesar, Hamlet, Othello, King Lear and Macbeth,* written c. 1596-1606 and in this order.

Structural Elements of Shakespearean Tragedy

All of Shakespeare's tragedies – as well as his comedies and histories – were divided into five acts by later editors. Each act is subdivided into varying numbers of scenes, which in turn differ considerably in length. The shortest scene in *Macbeth* has 10 lines (5.6), the longest 243 lines (4.3). A scene may be defined as a unit of action in which there is no change of place or break in the continuity of time (interval). At the end of a scene all characters leave the stage. As Elizabethan theatres had no curtain, such a 'clearing of the stage' was necessary. Shakespeare tended to juxtapose scenes differing in length as well as in other respects. Scenes may be private, public, official, ritual, ceremonial, intimate, comic etc.; likewise we may distinguish between expository, transitional, development, climactic, relief, messenger, monologue, dialogue, ensemble, forest, battle, balcony, street, garden, court, banquet, and chamber scenes.

Usually there is a movement from an initial situation of relative or at least seeming order through evil and crime towards a **crisis** characterized by disorder, confusion, chaos. The crisis is often emphasized by **correspondences** between human and cosmic spheres. It is close to the **turning point/peripety,** after which the opposing forces or the **antagonist** gain momentum and the powers of evil destroy themselves. After a final **catastrophe** the (initial) order is – at least seemingly – restored. This pattern can be described as a cyclical/ring structure. It may also be summarized in a diagram:

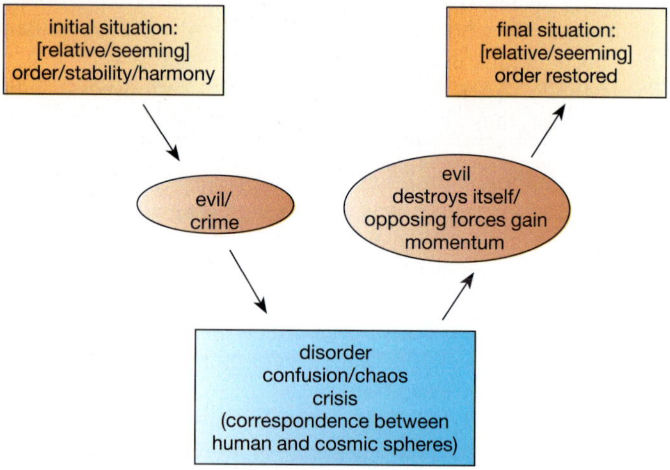

The tragic hero usually appears in the title role of the tragedy and has the longest part, with the exception of *Julius Caesar,* where Caesar is killed in 3.1, after he has spoken only 150 lines, whereas Brutus – seen by many as the really central figure and tragic hero – has 720 lines. By comparison: Macbeth has 705 lines, his wife 257, the whole tragedy 2349. The tragedy of *Hamlet* is nearly twice as long, with 4042 lines; its hero alone – one of the longest, most difficult, most admired roles in world literature – has no less than 1507 lines. (All figures according to Marvin Spevack's *Complete and Systematic Concordance to the Works of Shakespeare.)*

1. At which point in the play can you tell that there is not going to be a 'happy ending' for Macbeth? Discuss various central scenes for their function as turning-points of the action.
2. Look at the Wheel of Fortune on page 134 and mark the stages of Macbeth's rise and fall on its circumference. At which point is he at the zenith ['zenɪθ] of his power and can say 'regno'?

Shakespeare and 'his' Time: The Order of the World

When we talk about past times, the first difficulty we encounter is the necessity to give them names. 'Shakespeare's time' or 'Shakespeare's age' – though still very common – are misleading terms because they sound as if he had been the most important, most influential person who lived in England at the turn of the sixteenth into the seventeenth century, and he certainly was not. 'Elizabethan England' and 'Jacobean England' are more precise terms, taking the names of monarchs to characterize their times. When reading about Shakespeare, however, who was born under Elizabeth I and died under James I, you will find that in history books 'the Elizabethan age' conveniently encompasses almost a whole century, from 1558 to 1642. There are alternative ways of giving names to historical periods. 'Early modern England' (c. 1500 to c. 1800) is a neutral but rather vague label, used to describe long-term developments. Art-history prefers the term 'Renaissance', and this has been adopted by literary and cultural historians as well.

The **Renaissance** – the 're-birth' of classical Greek and Roman learning, resulting in a radical change of self-image and world-picture – reached England late. In Italy, the Renaissance is said to have begun around 1300, and it took about two hundred years to travel across Europe to England, where it arrived at roughly the same time as the Reformation and lasted until the middle of the seventeenth century.

Elizabethan England – which came to an end when King Charles I was executed by the order of his own parliament in 1649 – was a time in which order and disorder, stability and change, uniformity and multiplicity, were at war with one another. Any assessment of the age must comprehend one central *paradox: the more emphatically* and forcefully 'order' and 'stability' are affirmed in the texts that have come down to later generations (and there are a great many such texts from Elizabethan England), the more likely it is that the people who wrote these texts felt that their world was *dis*ordered and *un*stable. This *paradox is easy to understand. 'Please put your rubbish into the bins provided', 'Don't drive faster than 30 miles an hour', 'Pupils will walk calmly and quietly in the corridors' – all of these statements betray the fact that people *do* leave their rubbish anywhere, *do* drive as fast as they like, and *do* run screaming down school corridors. When Elizabethan voices of authority – clergymen, lawyers, politicians – tell their audiences that the world has been made and ordered by God, that everyone has his or her fixed place in it, that it would be a sin to aspire to be or to have something that is not yours by birth, they are trying to reassure themselves and others of the stability of a *status quo** that was always in danger of crumbling and dissolving.

emphatically strongly, with emphasis

status quo Lat.: the present state of things

One of the main reasons for these *ideological changes was the **secularization*** of society. Overseas colonialization gave Europeans a new sense of superiority, scientific inventions, commerce and money markets boomed, social mobility increased. It became more important to appear to advantage before your

secularization the process of making something secular, i.e. of this world (rather than the next world)

neighbours than before God. People wanted to achieve and live well in this world, not wait for reward in the next.
This idea of improving yourself and your lot in this world has been called **'Renaissance self-fashioning'**. Every man (women were largely excluded from this enterprise) was obliged to use his free will to make the best of himself:

> 'You shall fix the limits of your own nature according to the free choice in whose power I have placed you,' says God to man in a famous Renaissance treatise. 'We have made you neither mortal nor immortal, so that with freedom and honour you should be your own sculptor and maker, to fashion your form as you choose.'[1]

Attitudes towards **poverty** changed radically in the 200 years from 1400 to 1600: in the Middle Ages, people had seen much to admire in the poor, who were like Christ in his wretchedness. Early modern governments adopted a more rigid attitude: if you are poor, it is your own fault, because you are not trying hard enough to find work.

correspondence similarity, harmony

This new image of man as free and powerful posed new problems, however. The individual, determined to fashion himself according to his ideals and ambitions, was bound to come into conflict with society, particularly with the early modern national states, which were still struggling to centralize political power in the person of a monarch. Renaissance drama is full of tragic heroes who fail and die because they find it impossible to reconcile the demands of society with their personal desires and doubts.
Shakespeare's plays are set at all sorts of times, in all sorts of places – but never in Elizabethan England. Nevertheless, it can be assumed that he is always writing about his own time; there was no attempt to be historically correct about past ages. Macbeth's Scotland, too, must be understood in terms of Elizabeth's and James's England. One *ideological concept is particularly important here: the **correspondence* between microcosm and macrocosm.** The most frequent metaphors one finds in Renaissance political writing are those equating the human body, the state, and the universe. Nor were these merely figures of speech: it was believed (at least theoretically) that the order of the universe was, or should be, mirrored by the order of society and of the human body:

> 'For like as the body in every man receiveth his life by virtue of the soul and is governed thereby, so doth the multitude of people in every country receive, as it were, civil life by laws well administered by good officers and wise rulers, by whom they be governed and kept in politic order.'[2]

---

[1] Pico della Mirandola, *Oration on the Dignity of Man,* 1486.
[2] Thomas Starkey, *A Dialogue Between Cardinal Pole and Thomas Lupset,* 1534-5.

One of Shakespeare's characters sums up a related idea:

> 'The heavens themselves, the planets, and this centre
> Observe degree*, priority, and place [...]
> Office and custom, in all line of order.
> And therefore is the glorious planet Sol*
> In noble eminence enthroned and sphered [...]
> And posts like the commandment of a king,
> Sans check*, to good and bad. But when the planets
> In evil mixture to disorder wander,
> What plagues and what portents, what mutiny? [...]
> Take but degree away, untune that string,
> And hark what discord* follows.[3]

degree rank, hierarchy

Sol the sun

Sans check Without hindrance

discord disharmony

For those who profit from the *status quo*, this naturalization of the political and social order is very convenient: God is good; he has created nature and everything in it, therefore the existing order is good and natural, too. Any attempt to change it is wicked and sinful; and anyone who goes against the norms and rules is not only up against society but also against nature and, finally, against God.

1. Inform yourselves about the central, most far-reaching events in England and in Europe from c. 1500 to c. 1700, and link them to what you have learnt about this period in the above paragraphs.
2. To what effect is the Elizabethan concept of the correspondence between microcosm and macrocosm worked into the play *Macbeth?*
   a) Find passages or scenes in which characters refer to the correspondence between the natural and the political order.
   b) What ideas or feelings are they expressing with the help of this concept?
3. Take another look at the form and nature of Macbeth's ambition to become king. Is it fair to say that his rise and fall are an illustration of what can happen if the idea of 'self-fashioning' is carried to extremes?

[3] *Troilus and Cressida,* 1.3.85-110.

Glossary

Action the main events in a play; the chain of incidents linked by chronological or accidental connections. > **plot**

Allegiance [əˈliːdʒəns] the duty by a subject to his sovereign, sworn by an oath. (See context on *world order)*

Alliteration the repetition of initial (stressed) consonantal sounds, e.g. 'Fair ist foul'

Antithesis [ænˈtɪθəsɪs] a way of structuring a piece of writing by setting one character, thought, or idea against a contrasting one, not necessarily its opposite. Shakespeare's plays abound in antitheses, although sometimes they are not obvious. 'Win us with honest trifles, to betray's / In deepest consequence' (1.3.123-4) is a fairly straightforward double antithesis; but 'His silver skin laced with his golden blood' is not immediately recognized: the antithetical contrast results from the fact that where the skin is whole, the man is whole, but if the skin is cut open, blood appears and death follows.

Aside a remark or a short speech made by a dramatic character. It is a dramatic convention, i.e. a sort of agreement between author and audience, that the aside can only be heard by the audience and not by the characters surrounding the speaker on the stage. This may seem artificial but is in fact quite common in drama, especially so in *Macbeth*. The character of Macbeth is given a great number of asides by Shakespeare, which underlines his isolation and the fact that he tends to hide his feelings and ideas from others. > **soliloquy**

Assonance the repetition of identical or similar vowel sounds (the effect of which is comparable to that of > **alliteration**) e.g. '… we three meet …', 1.1.1, '… thrice … nine', 1.3.34

Blank verse unrhymed lines of ten (or eleven) syllables patterned in iambic pentameter. 'iambic' means that one foot consists of an unstressed and a stressed syllable; 'pentameter' means that one line has five feet (cf. p.120).

Characterization the fleshing-out of a dramatic figure to give it lifelike dimensions. Actors are very keen to make the parts they play as vivid and credible as possible; they pick up every hint and clue in the play in order to decide 'what sort of a person' their character might be. A playwright can characterize his or her figures either directly (i.e. by describing them in the > **stage directions**) or, more usually, by the way the figures speak, behave, and talk about each other. Indirect characterization is more interesting than direct characterization because it leaves more room for interpretation: The Captain says that Macbeth slices people in two without batting an eyelid; Lady Macbeth says that he is 'full o'the milk of human kindness'.

Chiasmus [kaɪˈæzməs] the opposite of > **parallelism,** the corresponding terms – often > **antitheses** – being arranged crosswise, e.g.: '… all hail Macbeth and Banquo.' – 'Banquo and Macbeth, all hail', 1.3.66 f.
'Sore labour's bath, Balm of hurt minds,' 2.2.42 f.
The term chiasmus is derived from the Greek letter chi = x.

Chorus/Choric scene In ancient Greek tragedies the Chorus is a group of persons who comment from time to time on the action and on the behaviour of the principal characters. It usually expresses commonsense attitudes of ordinary spectators, thus providing some sort of basic interpretation of a passage without influencing the action of the play. In *Macbeth* there are several such scenes.

Chronicles written accounts of the history of a nation. Shakespeare took the material for many of his history plays, including *Macbeth,* from Raphael Holinshed's *Chronicles of England, Scotland and Ireland* (1578). Chronicles of English history were enormously popular at Shakespeare's time; they bore a significant part in the shaping of English people's national consciousness and pride.

Comic relief a comic episode within a tragic context, often used to relieve tension or – on the contrary – to heighten by contrast the tragic emotion

Convention an agreement between an author and his readers/audience to accept an element in a work of literature or in art in general which differs from the reality it represents, e.g. > **soliloquies**, > **asides**; the stage standing for an open landscape, a battlefield, a room in a palace; verse or singing as a mode of expression, dancing in a ballet, abstractions in painting or sculpture.

Cross-dressing Also 'transvestism'. The practice of wearing clothes that are more usually reserved for members of the other sex. Dress codes in Elizabethan times were much stricter than they are today. To put on someone else's clothes meant, in a very real sense, to put on his or her identity, which was seen as a confusion of the existing political, social and sexual order.

Dilemma a situation which leaves only a choice between two equally unwelcome possibilities; e.g. in his soliloquy (1.7.1-28) Macbeth is torn between the consequences of killing a king and the frustration of his ambition to become a king.

Dramatic irony often synonymous with 'tragic irony', implying that a character is not fully aware of what he is saying, whereas the audience realizes the deeper significance of the statement. *Macbeth* contains many examples of this. The most famous one is probably when King Duncan, referring to the treacherous former Thane of Cawdor, states:
'There's no art to find the mind's construction in the face', 1.4.12 f.
In contrast to the audience, Duncan has no idea that this is particularly true of Macbeth, who is just entering, and whom Duncan mistakes to be his 'worthiest cousin', 1.4.14, although we feel that he will soon be his assassin. Dramatic or tragic irony must never be confused with > **verbal or rhetorical irony.**

Dumb show the silent, often stylized, enactment of a play's or a scene's > **action** before it was played out properly. Dumb shows were very popular in Elizabethan tragedies, although Shakespeare does not employ the device very often.

Edition Shakespeare did not write *Macbeth* in the form and shape in which you are holding it in your hands. The text of the play was prepared for a wide readership by an editor, who checked different versions of the play against each other, modernized the spelling, numbered the acts, scenes and lines. Many editions add textual notes to explain unfamiliar words.

Euphemism ['juːfəmɪzm] an indirect statement or circumlocution used to avoid bluntness or taboo words, e.g. the replacement of 'murder' by 'deed', 'thing', 'business'.

Gender a concept of masculinity and femininity that sees and explains them as socially constructed and mediated, not as 'naturally' given. People may be born male or female, but sexual differences in identity, behaviour, desires, etc. are implanted in them by education and society. Modern ideas about what a 'man' should be or what a 'woman' should be are in many ways (not in all) more relaxed and flexible than early modern ones. In Shakespeare's time, people's sense of 'identity' was more unstable and fluid than it is today; a person *was* what he or she *did,* so if a man behaved or acted in a way that was thought to be feminine, he lost his male identity and 'degenerated' into a woman.

Hyperbole [haɪ'pɜːbəlɪ] an exaggeration. Shakespeare often makes his characters use hyperbolical style, esp. when they are under stress, e.g.:
'Will all great Neptune's ocean wash this blood
Clean from my hand? No: this my hand will rather
The multitudinous seas incarnadine,
Making the green one red,' 2.2.63-66.
'... all the perfumes of Arabia will not sweeten this little hand,' 5.1.43 f.

Ideology [aɪdɪ'ɒlədʒɪ] the sets of beliefs characteristic of a social group, class, or individual about society, culture/religion, > **gender** relationships, politics, etc. Ideology determines people's conscious and subconscious ideas about identity, hierarchy, and power relations. This definition is wider and more comprehensive than the one you may be more familiar with, 'a declared commitment to political ideas seen as fanatical by the rest of society' (see con-text on *world order).*

Image a picture created in the mind by words, often used to make abstract notions more vivid. Shakespeare's characters continually express themselves through images or imagery, i.e. images taken collectively. If an image is used in connection with an adverb of comparison, it may be called a simile, e.g.:
'... his great love, sharp as his spur, ...' 1.6.24,
'... his virtues
Will plead like angels, trumped-tongued ...'
1.7.18 f.

For Banquo's issue have I filed my mind (3.1.66)

Otherwise it is a metaphor, often a > **personification**, e.g.: 'Bloody instructions ... being taught, return' (1.7.9).

Monosyllable a word consisting of one syllable only. These simple words, which are relatively frequent in English, tend to be very effective, especially when whole lines or more are made up exclusively of monosyllables, e.g.:
'Fair is foul, and foul is fair' 1.1.12.
'If it were done when 'tis done, then 'twere well
It were done ...' 1.7.1 f.
'That which hath made them drunk, hath made me bold; / What hath quenched them, hath ...' 2.2.1 f.
The polysyllabic (i.e. containing more than one syllable) words following such a series of monosyllables are often awaited in >**suspense** and thus also emphasised in their significance.

Onomatopoeia [ˌɒnəˌmætəˈpiːə] the attempt by the poet to match the sound of his words and sentences to their sense. Some words, like animal cries, are onomatopoetic in every language; but the poet strives for a special effect. The metre of verse is often helpful here: you can almost hear the weary, dragging footsteps of Time in Macbeth's famous 'Tomorrow, and tomorrow, and tomorrow / Creeps in this petty pace from day to day ...' (5.5.18-9).

Paradox a statement containing opposite ideas that make it seem absurd or unlikely although it is or may be true. The word is derived from Greek para doxa, i.e. contrary to accepted opinion, the opposite of orthodox, i.e. conform to what is generally accepted as right. *Macbeth* abounds in paradoxes, e.g.:
'Lesser than Macbeth, and greater.
Not so happy, yet much happier.' 1.3.63 f.
'... to win us to our harm, ...' 1.3.122
Whenever you see or hear a paradox, try to discover its hidden meaning.

Parallelism a sentence or other speech unit in which corresponding elements have the same or similar structures, e.g.:
'... Cannot be ill, cannot be good. If ill,
Why hath it ...
If good, why do I ...' 1.3.130 ff.

Personification a figure of speech in which things, animals, abstract ideas, etc. are treated as human beings, e.g.
'Come, thick night,
...That my keen knife see not the wound it makes,
Nor heaven peep through the blanket of the dark,
To cry, 'Hold, hold', 1.5.48 ff.

Plot plan or outline of events in a play; it tends to emphasize the causal development of the > **action** and to be more systematically arranged.

Pun wordplay involving words that sound similar but have different meanings. Puns are often light-hearted and amusing, but it is also an effective way of combining several aspects of the same thing: When Lady Macbeth says 'I'll gild the faces of the grooms withal, / For it must seem their guilt 2.2.59-60), she (probably subconsciously) links the ideas of a gold-red painted surface, deception, blood and regicide.
Shakespeare has been accused of not being able to resist even the silliest, flattest, most tasteless puns, but this criticism fails to appreciate the overflowing joy of language and its multiplicity that was shared by Elizabethan poets, playwrights and audiences alike.

Rhetoric [ˈretərɪk] the effective presentation of ideas in speech or writing. At medieval and early modern universities, rhetoric – based on classical Roman teaching – was an important discipline; every educated person was trained to express and arrange their arguments in the style appropriate for the subject matter. The aim of the rhetorician was to convince and persuade his audience of his arguments, which meant that he had to work on their intellectual understanding as well as on their emotions and imagination.

Rhyme repetition of all sounds following the last stressed vowel in words at the ends of lines. If one such line follows the other immediately, we have a rhyming **couplet,** which is often used to mark the end of a scene or to underline an utterance. It is opposed to > **blank verse.** Examples of rhyming couplets marking the ends of scenes **and** putting emphasis on final sentences:
'Away, and mock the time with fairest show,
False face must hide what the false heart does know' 1.7.80-1.
'Hear it not, Duncan, for it is a knell
That summons thee to heaven or to hell' 2.1.63-4.
The witches tend to emphasise their magic language by internal rhyme and > **assonance**:
'Thrice to thine, and thrice to mine' 1.3.35.

Enter Lady Macbeth with a tapir (5.1.15 SD)

Soliloquy [sə'lɪləkwɪ] derived from Latin *solus* + *loqui,* sometimes used as a synonym of 'monologue', derived from Greek *monos* + *logos.* Both terms mean that one character is alone on stage, talking either directly to the audience or to himself or herself (and thus only indirectly to the audience). As a rallying or moralizing address to the audience, it is a convention of medieval drama. Elizabethan playwrights, Shakespeare in particular, turned the character's attention inwards: the speaker voices his or her secret > **dilemmas,** observations and intentions and thus reveals them to the audience. Macbeth is an extreme example of a character who seems to have no desire at all to share his thoughts and feelings with the audience. See also > **aside.**

Stage business the gestures, movements and other nonverbal actions with which actors accompany their lines. It can range from eleborate set-ups with many props and music to little gestures like smiles, touches or the lighting of a cigarette.

Stage directions (SDs) those parts of the text of a play that are not to be spoken by the characters but serve as instructions to actors and directors as to the tone or looks of a character, the set-up of the stage, music, etc. While the SDs in 19th-century plays often read like extracts from a novel, Elizabethan playwrights restricted themselves to a minimum: sometimes they only list all speaking characters at the beginning of a scene and leave the actors to work out everything for themselves, including the exact moments of their entrances and exits.

Stage set the scenery and furniture on stage to specify the setting of a scene. There were practically no sets in Elizabethan plays; at most one finds a throne (to signify a king's palace) or a bed (to signify a bedroom) or a table and chairs (to signify a tavern).

Subtext the underlying, unexpressed meaning, opinion or theme in a remark or conversation. Examples from everyday life are easy to find: 'You've been to the hairdresser's, haven't you?' [= 'Your hair looks awful.'] or 'No, of course I don't mind driving you to the station in the middle of the night!' [= 'Leave me alone, you lazy so-and-so!'] In order to understand the subtext in a conversation, one usually has to know the speakers and their relationship quite well.

Suspense/tension these two words have overlapping meanings and are usually translated by the same word into German. In English it is useful to differentiate: tension exists above all between opposing forces, e.g. neighbouring countries, government and opposition, Macbeth and his lady; suspense, on the other hand, implies a feeling of uncertainty about what is going to happen next. It is characteristic of crime stories and also of *Macbeth.*

Tetrameter [tə'træmɪtə]a verse line in tetrameter has only four feet. The Weird Sisters in *Macbeth* speak in iambic tetrameter: 'But in a sieve I'll thither sail, / And like a rat without a tail …' (1.1.7-8). > **Blank verse**.

Theme a central or dominating idea in a play or other work of art. Important themes in *Mac-*

beth are ambition, appearance vs. reality, evil, order vs. chaos, the reversal of values, tyranny, violence, war.

Tone results from the speaker's attitude towards his subject and the other characters on stage. It may be serious, solemn, formal, dignified, etc. or comic, ironic, detached, playful, etc. and thus determine the atmosphere of a passage.

Verbal irony In its simplest form, the speaker says the direct opposite of what he really means. At the same time he makes it quite clear to his listener/s that he is intentionally being ironical; e.g.: when the Captain praising Macbeth's and Banquo's valour in 1.2. is asked by King Duncan whether the two war heroes were 'dismayed' by their Norwegian enemies, the answer is 'Yes, ...', 1.2.35. But by adding 'as sparrows, eagles, or the hare, the lion' the Captain 'signals', i.e. he makes it clear that Macbeth and Banquo were indeed no more afraid than eagles or lions are of sparrows and hares, i.e. not at all. Thus everybody will understand that 'yes' in this context means 'no'. There are much more complex and subtle forms of verbal or rhetorical irony, which must never be confused with > **dramatic irony**.

Wheel of Fortune/Rota Fortunae human life has always been regarded as a series of ups and downs. Especially in the Middle Ages and not much less in Shakespeare's time this fact was represented in the symbol of a wheel continually turned round by the goddess Fortuna. Men considered themselves to be linked to that wheel, which thus served as a warning to high-ranking persons and as a symbol of hope to people in misery. The theme of the 'Fall of Princes' was for a long time the central idea of tragedy. It is also relevant in *Macbeth,* where the tragic hero first moves upward, before he rapidly falls to his final destruction. On the other hand, the turning of the wheel appears as a consolation and an encouragement to the opposing forces: 'Things at the worst will cease, or else climb upward/To what they were before' 4.2.14 f.
So on the wheel (illustration) you see four times the same figure: on the left, moving upward, he says 'regnabo' (I shall govern), on top: 'regno' (I am governing), falling down: 'regnavi' (I used to govern), and finally: 'sum sine regno' (I am without kingdom, i.e. no longer king). In the middle of the wheel you see the goddess Fortuna turning the weel without herself being moved. For the meaning of the inscription round the wheel – 'Fortun(a)e Rota volvitur: Descendo minoratus. Alter in altum tollitur, nimis exaltatus' – ask your Latin teacher.

For Further Thinking

Six weeks after the coronation of Malcolm as new King of Scotland: Donaldbain and his wife are sitting at breakfast (Tea is not available, nobody in Scotland yet has an idea that there is such a place as India). Donaldbain has dreamt he was Malcolm's elder brother and should have inherited the crown. Write a dialogue for the couple.

Coming full circle

'The time is free.' From a BBC film (1982)

Macduff is now Malcolm's top security adviser and commander-in-chief of Scotland's armed forces. His secret dream is to conquer England. One of his spies, who eavesdropped on the Donaldbain couple's conversation, has just delivered a report on this. Macduff wants more money from King Malcolm to increase the size of his army. How does he proceed? Remember how much he knows and that he might feel that he put Malcolm on the throne in the first place.

Power games

The real **Donald Ban** (1033-97) followed his brother Malcolm (1031-93, King: 1058-93) on the throne in 1093. But he was soon deposed by Malcolm's son, named Duncan II after his grandfather. Donald Ban then combined forces with his cousin Edmund, defeated and killed Duncan II in 1094, after which they governed together for a while, until they were opposed and defeated by Edmund's brother Edgar, who blinded and imprisoned Donald Ban for life. As a reprisal, Edmund strangled his brother Edgar's eldest son to death … rough times … when the going gets tough the tough get going. What do you call this figure of speech?

Acknowledgements

Illustrations

p. 4: © John Tramper; p. 5: Illustration: Paul Cox, photo: © Richard Kalina; p. 7: Tate Gallery, London; p. 8, 14 bottom, 22: BBC 2/Canadian Broadcasting 1976; NDR HBG 1981: Verdi, Macbeth; p. 11: Robert Harding Picture Library; p. 14 top, 21, 31, 74, 93 top left,102, 105, 118, 134: Verlagsarchiv Schöningh; p. 18, 19: taken from: Roger Manvell: Shakespeare and the Film. London: J.M. Dent & Sons Ltd. 1971; p. 25: Rainer Gocke/Verlagarchiv Schöningh; p. 26, 40, 135: © BBC Enterprises Ltd. 1988; p. 28: City of Manchester Art Galleries; p.-29, 36, 39, 45, 57: Photographs of the 1955 Stratford-upon-Avon production *Macbeth* by Angus McBean, in the Harvard Theatre Collection, Harvard University, Cambridge, Mass.; p. 33 top left: Requet, Paris; p. 33 bottom left: Colorific, London; p. 33 right: © Cinetext, Frankfurt; p. 41, 46 left: Art Collection of the Folger Shakespeare Library, Washington, D.C.; p. 46 right, 96 top left: © Thames Television Ltd 1978; p. 48: © By Courtesy Of The Dean And Chapter Of Westminster, London; p. 50: UP/Corbis Images; p. 51, 60, 71, 82, 96 bottom left, 106: Copyright © 1971 Playboy Productions and Columbia Pictures Industries, Inc.; p. 53: National Film Archive Stills Library; p. 63: Victoria & Albert Museum, London; p. 65: Engraving in: George Turberville, The Noble Art of Venerie, 1575; p. 72 top left: Illustration for Time by Stephen Bliss; p. 72 bottom left, p.89 (2 photos, left and right): © dpa, Frankfurt; p. 72 right: © Hessischer Rundfunk; p. 76: The Shakespeare Centre Library, Stratford-upon-Avon; p.-79: J. Freeman; p. 85: Scode Editrice, Mailand; p. 89 left: Bologna, Pinacoteca Nazionale; p. 93 top right, 93 bottom: taken from: Stephen Orgel: Impersonations. The performance of gender in Shakespeare's England. Cambridge: Cambridge University Press 1996; p. 94 left: TM & © 1997 Lucasfilm Ltd.; p. 94 bottom: Bildarchiv Preußischer Kulturbesitz, Berlin; p. 96 right: Reg Wilson; p. 107: Artificial Eye; p. 121: Guildhall Library, City of London; p. 123: C. Walter Hodges, 1965

Every effort has been made to supply complete copyright information for the pictures included here. Should such entries be incomplete or contain errors, we request copyright owners to contact the publishers so that we can proceed with the necessary corrections and/or customary compensation.

Texts

All „Con-Texts" written by Rainer Gocke and Angela Stock.